TYPE 2 DIABETES COOKBOOK FOR BEGINNERS

Take Control of Your Health Naturally, With **1800+ Days** of Delicious and Affordable Recipes. Manage Blood Sugar and Improve A1C With a **28-day Meal Plan** For Beginners and Advanced users in This Guide.

By Zachary Tibaldi

Table of Contents

Introduction

Managing type 2 diabetes may be challenging, but with the guidance of this book, you can produce delicious, nutritious meals for the rest of your life that will both aid in diabetes management and make you want to cook them again and again.

One of the primary concerns of those who have been diagnosed with type 2 diabetes is their nutrition. You'll probably have a never-ending stream of tasks thrown at you. Making and keeping medical appointments, taking medications, giving up bad habits like smoking and isolation, and eating a healthy, well-rounded diet might all seem like a lot to handle. It might be challenging to know what to do when there is so much to learn and so many myths to dispel about diabetes and eating.

Type 2 diabetes is a metabolic condition that having trouble regulating and using sugar (glucose) as fuel. This persistent (chronic) illness causes an abnormally high concentration of glucose in the blood.

Type 2 diabetes may be controlled with lifestyle changes such as dieting, exercise, and weight loss. If food and exercise aren't cutting it when it comes to managing your blood sugar, it may be time to consider diabetes medication or insulin treatment.

Although a healthy diet is essential for keeping blood sugar levels stable, just because you have diabetes does not mean you have to give up all your favorite flavors. In fact, it's recommended that you consume nutrient-dense meals that have a range of carbohydrate types, protein sources, and fat types.

For those struggling with Type 2 diabetes, the recipes in this book are a healthy way to feel more in charge of their eating habits and less stressed about their health. This book is a great resource for anybody with diabetes or at risk of getting the condition since it details the best preventative measures and treatment options.

Even if you have type 2 diabetes, you may still have a delicious lunch. With the information in this book, you can prepare a dinner that will not only satisfy your appetite but also help you control your type 2 diabetes.

You may find it easier to control your diabetes if you adhere to your medication schedule, attend your doctor's visits, and learn about and get assistance for diabetes self-management. Both diet and exercise play an important role in maintaining good health for those with diabetes. Maintaining a healthy level of blood glucose, commonly known as blood sugar, may be accomplished by eating a balanced diet and engaging in regular physical activity.

If you have type 2 diabetes and are looking to improve your diet, this book is for you. Our go-to recipes for maintaining a balanced diet and lifestyle while managing diabetes are collected here.

Type-2 Diabetes: What Is It?

Damage to the body's capacity to regulate and utilize sugar (glucose) as fuel is at the root of type 2 diabetes, a metabolic illness. An abnormally high level of glucose (sugar) circulates in the blood because of this persistent (ongoing) disease. Long-term damage to the cardiovascular, neurological, and immunological systems may result from uncontrolled blood sugar levels.

Two related diseases are responsible for the development of type 2 diabetes. You reduce your sugar intake because your pancreas is not producing enough of the hormone insulin, which controls how fast sugar enters your cells.

Although both types of diabetes may manifest at any age, type 2 diabetes is more typically thought of as an adult-onset condition. While older people are more likely to develop type 2 diabetes, rising childhood obesity rates have led to an uptick in cases in younger age groups.

Type 2 diabetes may be controlled with lifestyle changes such as dieting, exercising, and losing weight. You may need to take diabetes medicine or undergo insulin therapy if you have trouble maintaining a healthy blood sugar level via food and exercise alone.

But your body starts to ignore insulin when you have Type 2 diabetes, and glucose builds up in your bloodstream instead of being utilized for energy. Increased blood glucose levels, comparable to those seen in Type 1 diabetes, come from insulin resistance.

The pancreas goes into overdrive in the onset phases of Type 2 diabetes, producing excessive amounts of insulin in an effort to counteract insulin resistance. Pancreatic insulin production declines with age. So, some people with Type 2 diabetes have to inject insulin for a very long time, much as those with Type 1 diabetes.

Symptoms of type 2 diabetes often emerge gradually and may remain undiagnosed for quite some time (sometimes, there are no apparent symptoms). Due to the insidious nature of the disease, anybody with any of these risk factors should see their doctor to have their blood sugar monitored.

You may be at risk for type 2 diabetes if:

- You have prediabetes.
- You are overweight.
- You have a parent, brother, or sister with type 2 diabetes.
- You lead a sedentary life with little or no physical activity

- Are older than 45 years.
- You have had gestational diabetes (during pregnancy)
- You have nonalcoholic fatty liver disease

Nearly one in ten Americans, or more than 34 million people, have diabetes, the vast majority of whom have type 2. It typically manifests in adults over the age of 45 after a protracted period of development. (But also at younger ages, such as newborns and teens).

By making positive changes to one's lifestyle, eating habits, and level of physical activity, type 2 diabetes may be prevented or at least put on hold.

The majority of people with type 2 diabetes are adults. On the other hand, children and adolescents who are overweight are more likely to develop Type 2 diabetes at a younger age.

Signs & Symptoms

It's possible that the signs of type 2 diabetes won't be recognized since they're so mild. Around 8 million people have it without knowing it.

- Having a severe thirst
- A constant need to go to the bathroom
- Vision blurred
- Having a short temper
- Numbness and tingling in your limbs
- Weakness or exhaustion

- Non-healing wounds
- Persistent yeast infections
- Irresistible hunger
- Loss of body fat without dieting
- Developing subsequent infections

See a doctor immediately if you see a black rash on your neck or underarms. Acanthosis nigricans is a skin disease that may indicate insulin resistance.

Causes

The pancreas secretes a hormone called insulin. It helps your body turn the sugar glucose found in meals into energy. Insulin is produced in the bodies of people with type 2 diabetes, but it is not used properly by the body's cells. Initially, your pancreas will create extra insulin to help shuttle glucose into your cells. Yet, it loses the ability to sustain this process, leading to a buildup of glucose in the blood.

In most cases, a number of risk factors work together to bring on type 2 diabetes. They could include the following elements:

- Genes: Many Genetic regions have been identified that control insulin production in the body.
- Additional mass: Carrying additional weight around the middle, which is common among the overweight and obese, increases the risk of developing insulin resistance.

- When the body's metabolism is thrown off, a condition known as metabolic syndrome develops: Symptoms of insulin resistance include but are not limited to hyperglycemia, hypertension, abdominal fat, elevated cholesterol, and elevated triglycerides.
- When your blood sugar drops too low, your liver starts making and releasing glucose: It goes up after you eat, and your liver tends to slow down and store the glucose for later. Nonetheless, some individuals still manufacture sugar and do not engage in this practice.
- There is a breakdown in cellular communication: It is possible for cells to send out faulty signals or to misinterpret incoming information. If any of these factors affect your cells' ability to generate or utilize insulin or glucose, you may develop diabetes.
- A damaged beta cell: If the cells in your body that produce insulin release the wrong amount of insulin at the wrong time, your blood sugar will be thrown off. This damage might be caused by high blood sugar levels as well.

What Does It Mean to Have Type 2 Diabetes?

A diagnosis of type 2 diabetes does not reflect a moral failing on the part of the patient. It's not because of anything you did wrong. And it doesn't imply you deserve punishment or condemnation.

Those who drink as much as you do, eat as much as you do, and watch as much television as you don't all end up with diabetes. This indicates that they are not part of your genetic makeup. The risk genes for getting diabetes may have been passed down to you from your parents or ancestors.

While there is a substantial hereditary component to type 2 diabetes, it is not a given that you will also have the condition. Genetics has a lesser role than other lifestyle variables like food and exercise. Type 2 diabetes-causing gene alterations may be affected by lifestyle factors such as diet and physical activity. Individuals who have a family history of diabetes should be wary of engaging in risky behaviors, including a sedentary lifestyle and bad eating habits. They, too, could get diabetes.

Type 2 diabetes is generally diagnosed when a battery of blood testing shows abnormalities. Increased levels of blood sugar are a hallmark of diabetes. This indicates that both your pre-meal (fasting) blood sugar and your post-prandial (two-hour post-meal) blood sugar levels are high.

Glucose, a type of sugar, is present in everyone's blood. Your body's cells get their energy from this source. Glucose is an essential food since it is the sole fuel source for your brain.

Of carbohydrates, glucose is the simplest. Glucose is found in almost all sources of carbohydrates. To fuel your body, your digestive system breaks down complex carbohydrates like bread, potatoes, rice, and pasta and refined sugars like the white crystals you pour into your coffee.

Glucose is taken into circulation from the intestines, which causes an increase in blood sugar levels. A fasting blood sugar level of around 5 mmol/L is considered normal. After eating, it usually goes up by approximately two points, reaching around 7 mmol per liter.

As blood sugar levels rise, the pancreas releases insulin. The insulin binds to insulin receptors, which are present in every cell in the body. It acts like a key, opening the cells to let glucose in. As it reaches our cells, it is put to use in metabolic reactions that provide the energy that keeps us going. This causes blood sugar to revert to pre-meal levels.

Normal variations in blood sugar occur at this rate. Each cycle should conclude in roughly four hours. What you consume and how much you exercise will define your whole fate. It's flexible in terms of length.

When diabetic, the pattern shifts. Your post-meal reading is likely to increase by more than two points, and your fasting reading is likely to be over 5 mmol per liter.

Chapter 1: Foods to Avoid and the Best Foods for Diabetes

What Are the Healthiest Foods to Include in Your Diet?

While living with diabetes, a nutritious diet and regular exercise are musts. Maintaining a healthy blood glucose (or sugar) level is only one of many health advantages that may come from eating well and doing regular exercise. Your blood glucose levels may be managed with a combination of diet, exercise, and, if required, medication for diabetes.

It might be less daunting to start slowly and get help from loved ones and medical professionals.

The good news is that you can keep eating all of your usual meals; the bad news is that you may have to reduce your serving sizes or cut down on how often you eat them. Diabetic patients may work with their healthcare providers to develop a personalized eating plan.

Maintaining a healthy weight and steady blood sugar levels are two additional benefits of eating sensibly. The number of calories you need to consume daily is something that your healthcare team can assist you with.

For certain diabetics, maintaining a regular eating schedule is essential. Some people could be more flexible with regard to when they eat. Depending on the kind of insulin you take or the type of diabetes medicine you take, you may need to eat the same number of carbohydrates at the same time every day. Using "mealtime" insulin will allow you to eat whenever you want. While using insulin or other diabetes treatments, skipping meals might cause a dangerously low blood sugar level.

Foods to Eat

Vegetables

Adding a meal rich in vegetables is the best solution for all diabetic patients.

The most recommended are:

- Spinach
- Cauliflower
- Broccoli
- Artichoke
- Tomatoes
- Asparagus

- Garlic
- Spring onions
- Onions
- Lemons
- Ginger

They are the ones that have a lower amount of carbohydrates.

Fruits

Some fruits contain a high amount of sugar in the form of sucrose and fructose and should be avoided.

The most recommended are:

- Apples
- Pears
- Berries
- Grapefruit
- Kiwi
- Bananas
- Cherries
- Grapes
- Orange
- Plums
- Peaches
- Nectarines
- Avocados

Nuts and Seeds

Nuts and seeds are highly recommended in a diabetic's diet because they are rich in macronutrients without fear of glucose spikes.

- Walnuts
- Peanuts
- Pecans
- Almonds
- Pistachios
- Sunflower seeds
- Pumpkin seeds
- Sesame seeds

Meat, Fish, and Seafood

You have to prefer white meat, such as poultry, fish, and seafood. Red meat is not banned, but it is better to eat it in moderation.

The most recommended are:

- Chicken
- Turkey
- All fish (salmon, trout, cod, halibut, sardines, etc.)
- Scallops
- Shrimp
- Oysters
- Mussels

Cereals

Try to minimize the amount of starch and prefer whole grains to refined grains, such as:

- Oats
- Quinoa
- Multigrain
- Whole grains
- Brown rice
- Millet
- Barley
- Sorghum
- Tapioca

Fats

Fat intake is the most debated topic regarding diet for diabetics. There are diets, such as the ketogenic diet, that is high in fat, but these are effective for diabetic patients. However, give preference to unsaturated fats.

The most recommended are:

- Olive oil
- Sesame oil
- Canola oil
- Grapeseed oil
- Other vegetable oils
- Fats extracted from plant sources

Dairy Products

Prefer low-fat dairy products such as:

- Skim milk
- Low-fat cheese
- Yogurt
- Margarine or butter without trans fats

Sugar substitutes can be a lifesaver for diabetics' recipes, as they bring no calories to the next meal and help to further lower blood glucose levels. Remember, however, that although sugar substitutes seem like a perfect solution, they still count as extra calories in the long run.

Stevia is the sweetest and should be used most carefully. Instead of 1 cup of sugar, 1 tsp of Stevia is sufficient; all other sweeteners are more or less similar to sugar in the intensity of sweetness.

Foods to Avoid

It is just as important to know which foods to avoid as it is to know which foods to include in a diabetic diet. This is due to the high carbohydrate and added sugar content of many meals and beverages, which can cause blood sugar levels to spike. Other foods may be harmful to your heart's health or cause weight gain. If you have diabetes, you should avoid the following foods.

Grain Refinement

White bread, pasta, and rice are high in carbohydrates but low in fiber, potentially causing blood sugar levels to rise faster than whole grains. However, one study found that whole-grain rice was far more effective than white rice at stabilizing blood sugar levels after eating.

Alcoholic Beverages

Alcohol is noteworthy since the quantity drank has a direct correlation to the impact on blood sugar levels. A small amount of alcohol, for instance, may cause a modest increase in blood sugar levels. Your blood sugar will plummet after drinking more since depression is a feature of the central nervous system and metabolism. Nevertheless, when your blood sugar drops dangerously low, and you're on the edge of a hypoglycemic crisis, things become tricky. The need to eat everything in sight is overwhelming. As a result, you'll be tempted to eat unhealthy meals like those heavy in carbs, artificial ingredients, and the like.

It is often recommended that people with diabetes abstain from alcohol entirely. This is because alcohol, particularly when ingested first thing in the morning, may produce a rapid drop in blood sugar.

Breakfast Cereal

Most morning cereals include a lot of sugar. Some brands have the same amount of sugar in a single serving as some desserts. When shopping for cereal, make sure you read the nutrition label carefully and choose a low-sugar kind. Alternatively, use oats and naturally sweeten them with a little fresh fruit.

Candy

Each serving of candy contains a lot of sugar. It often has a high glycemic index, likely to trigger blood sugar spikes and falls after eating.

Fruit Juice

Although 100% fruit juice can be consumed in moderation, it is preferable to stick to whole fruit whenever possible if you have diabetes. While fruit juice has all the carbohydrates and sugar present in fresh fruit, it lacks the fiber required to help balance blood sugar levels.

Canned Soups

They contain an incredible number of artificial substances that will destroy your metabolism. Avoid them at all costs, even if they seem very healthy or they have a low level of carbohydrates and so on, because they generally get included in the processed foods category.

Conventional Dairy

This one should also be avoided. This is because traditional dairy, such as that found in supermarkets and health food stores, are usually pasteurized, which kills all of the beneficial bacteria and microorganisms. Aside from that, they add a lot of sugar and artificial sweeteners to make it sweeter and more palatable and to keep their customers coming back for more.

Flavored Coffee Drinks

Though coffee is delicious, flavored coffee contains a lot of carbohydrates, which cause blood sugar to rise. Go for plain coffee instead of the Caramel Frappuccino.

Sodas

They are terrible because they contain a truckload of sugar, artificial sweeteners, and other ingredients that contribute to the diabetes epidemic that we are experiencing in our daily lives. When it comes to drinks, just avoid them at all costs. Only drink water, and if you can find it, coconut water. Tea, but unsweetened tea. As much as possible, avoid alcohol and soda.

Vegetable Oil

These are some of the most dangerous foods you can ever eat. Canola oil, crude corn oil, soy oil, and other vegetable oils are examples. The oils that are recommended are simply coconut oil and cocoa oil. Please avoid using any other oils. These vegetable oils not only harm your metabolism but also impair digestion, which contributes to poor blood sugar management.

Chapter 2: Proper Management of Medications and Dietary Supplements

Diabetes poses a serious danger to human life. Keeping to your diabetic treatment plan takes a commitment of twenty-four hours. Your efforts are nonetheless admirable. You may prevent significant, even fatal, outcomes by managing your diabetes.

Take Supplements

Doctors advise people with prediabetes and diabetes to eat a nutritious diet and exercise regularly, and they place little emphasis on the use of dietary supplements in their treatment. Fortunately, many supplements can help with both symptom relief and overall health and well-being. Always consult with your doctor before using any nutritional supplement, as not all supplement combinations are suitable for everyone. Some may interact with current medications or increase the likelihood of developing new health problems.

Some useful supplements for diabetes management are listed below.

Chromium Picolinate

According to one study, it aids in the binding of insulin to cell walls, making glucose absorption by insulin receptors easier. This results in lower blood glucose levels. The chromium content offers the same benefits as the chromium picolinate mentioned earlier.

Pycnogonid, an antioxidant, has been shown in studies to lower blood pressure, lower cholesterol, and regulate blood glucose levels. Recent research has shown that alpha-lipoic acid is critical in ensuring that insulin functions properly.

Magnesium

It is a mineral that is essential for lowering blood pressure. It also aids in the regulation of pulse rate, muscle function, and blood glucose levels. The recommended daily intake is 400 mg, and it's worth noting that many natural foods contain high concentrations of minerals. Consider the following scenarios: A half cup of spinach contains 75 mg of magnesium, while one ounce of dry-roasted almonds contains 80 mg.

Vitamin D

Currently, research is being conducted to determine whether its supplementation may reduce the risk of diabetes in children. It has also been shown to lower blood glucose levels in diabetics. Diabetes is also treated with it.

Asian Ginseng

This herb has been demonstrated to help reduce blood glucose levels in people with diabetes.

Curry Leaves

According to a study, consuming these leaves may be an effective weight-loss tool, which is especially beneficial for obese persons at risk of developing diabetes.

Stay Active

Even fifteen minutes of physical activity per day can have a significant impact on your overall health. However, if you are currently living an unhealthy lifestyle, even fifteen minutes may seem excessive. When most people think of exercise, they envision steamy gyms or sweaty, agitated people, and these are not images that inspire people to engage in physical activity. Is it possible to have a fitness plan for life if physical activity is not your thing? Yes, such a thing exists.

The key to becoming more interested in a fitness program is to shift your focus away from exercising and toward becoming more active. To be physically active, you do not need to be in training for a sport or attend an organized exercise class; all that is required is that you move. If you've spent the previous few years ignoring the need to move around by relying on labor-saving devices and technologies, it only takes getting out of your couch and walking around your house for a few minutes to start reaping the health benefits of being physically active.

You don't need any special equipment to get started, but it's important to wear comfortable shoes that won't pinch or irritate your feet as you walk. The more frequently you walk, the faster your body will adapt to the additional demands placed on it by the environment. This means that the more you walk, the better you become at walking.

In certain cases, you may discover that your 10-minute walk route is completed in just 5 minutes and that you can walk faster and farther while keeping a moderate level of exertion.

Swimming is another easy option to increase your physical activity if you have access to a pool.

Cycling is a terrific way to be active while also getting some exercise and fresh air at the same time.

Most Popular Medications for Type 2 Diabetes

- Metformin is the first medication that is usually prescribed. It improves the efficiency with which your body uses insulin. Nausea and diarrhea are possible side effects. These usually fade as your body adjusts to them.

- Pioglitazone: An anti-diabetic medication used in conjunction with a proper diet and exercise routine to control high blood sugar levels. To control glucose levels, it can be used alone or in combination with other medications. Sore throat, muscle pain, and weight gain are all possible side effects as your body adjusts to the medication. It is critical to notify your doctor if any side effects persist or worsen.

- Sitagliptin: An anti-diabetic medication that improves blood sugar control by increasing insulin release, particularly after a meal. It has the potential to reduce the amount of sugar produced by the liver.

- Exenatide is an anti-diabetic medication that aids in the release of insulin. It also slows food digestion and reduces the amount of sugar absorbed. Nausea, vomiting, diarrhea, and nervousness are all possible side effects as your body adjusts to the medication.

- Sulfonylureas: These aid in the production of insulin by the body. Low blood sugar and weight gain are two possible side effects.

- Meglitinides: These work similarly to sulfonylureas, but they are faster and have a shorter duration of action. They can cause side effects as well, but the risk is lower than with other medications.

- Thiazolidinediones: These are similar to metformin, but doctors usually do not recommend them because of the risk of heart failure and fractures.

- DPP-4 Inhibitors: These aid in the reduction of blood sugar levels. They have a minor effect but do not result in weight gain.

- GLP-1 Receptor Agonists: Not to be used alone. These medications help to lower blood sugar levels by slowing digestion.

- SGLT2 Inhibitors: This is one of the newest drugs for type 2 diabetes on the market. It prevents the kidneys from reabsorbing sugar into the blood, causing it to be excreted instead in the urine. Urinary infections and increased urination are two possible side effects.

- Insulin Therapy: Most people with type 1 diabetes must inject insulin, but some people with type 2 diabetes may also need insulin. The dosage and number of injections needed depend on each person, and your doctor will prescribe what is best for you.

Natural & Organic Medication

Herbs for diabetes are available to people nowadays. Specialists within this area have believed for years that diabetes can be managed with herbal medications. In fact, the effectiveness of those medicines continues to be ranked as amazing. The best part is that these herbs are non-toxic and are effective in fighting off and managing type 2 diabetes. However, it is always recommended to consult your doctor before starting any medication.

Here are a few of the popular natural medications that can handle diabetes efficiently:

- Pterocarpus marsupium: This medication is a distinctive mixture of herbs, such as Indian kino, Venge, Malabar kino, and Pita Sara. It has been used to heal diabetes for several years now.
- Bitter melon (Momordica Charania): Bitter melon, also called balsam pear, is a plant grown extensively in Asia, South America, and Africa. This folk medicine consists of various substances that are super rich in antibiotic qualities. However, it should not be given to individuals in large amounts.
- Gymnema Sylvestre: This plant is effective in assisting the pancreas to produce insulin in case of diabetes. In addition, it boosts the ability of insulin to lessen blood sugar levels and also reduces the desire for sweets. The plant can be an excellent replacement for medicines that reduce blood sugar levels in diabetics.
- Onion: This might be very hard for some to believe, but it is true. Onion substantially reduces blood sugar levels.

Develop Good Dietary Habits

Not just sugar and processed carbohydrates, but all carbs boost insulin release. There is conflicting evidence that the risk of diabetes is related to a diet's increase in blood sugar, even though refined carbohydrates are absorbed more quickly than complex carbohydrates.

Hence, controlling total carb consumption and choosing high-fiber carbohydrates are more effective strategies for preventing diabetes than limiting highly processed carbs.

Examples of foods and beverages that are rich in added sugar or refined carbohydrates include soda, candy, dessert, white bread, spaghetti, and sweetened morning cereal.

Broccoli, mushrooms, whole fruit, oats, whole-grain bread, and pasta are some examples of non-starchy foods that may stand in for grains. The increased fiber content of these meals aids in maintaining steady blood sugar levels.

Choosing water as your main beverage is a great way to cut down on your intake of sugary drinks.

Without treatment, dehydration may lead to long-term renal impairment, which manifests as headaches, lethargy, and an inability to concentrate. Daily water loss occurs from the breakdown of meals. Thus it's important to drink enough water throughout the day. Drinking enough water is the quickest and easiest approach to do this.

Carbohydrates from vegetables have the added benefit of keeping your water levels high because of the high-water content of most fruits and vegetables.

Drinking a daily green smoothie is a great way to get your greens and increase your hydration levels, and many people find that it is also a good way to get their greens and receive their antioxidants.

A green smoothie that contains at least 60% vegetables and no more than 40% fruit is an ideal combination for limiting the effects of the glycemic index. Here are a few examples of tasty food combinations that are also good for you:

Banana's natural sweetness complements the earthiness of the spinach and makes for an anti-oxidant-rich beverage.

Kale has several important nutrients, including vitamin C, calcium, iron, and beta-carotene.

But citrus fruits like kiwis and oranges are loaded with vitamin C and are a great way to get your daily dose of antioxidants.

Apples, pears, bananas, and dates are tossed with collard greens in this salad. Dates are high in iron and calcium, and collard greens are a good source of omega-3 fatty acids.

Sugary drinks, such as soda and sweetened fruit juice, have been linked to the development of type 2 diabetes and latent autoimmune diabetes in adults.

On the other side, it has been suggested that increased water intake may lead to better blood sugar management and insulin response.

Consuming a diet high in fiber may aid in digestive health and weight reduction. Maybe, it can help keep diabetes at bay, too.

Patients with prediabetes and overweight or obese older women may benefit from this vitamin since it aids in keeping blood sugar and insulin levels stable.

There are two different kinds of fiber: soluble fiber, which can soak up liquid, and insoluble fiber, which cannot.

Soluble fiber and water combine in the digestive system to form a gel that slows down the rate at which sugar is absorbed. Hence, it may be possible to reduce fasting blood sugar and insulin levels by increasing soluble fiber intake.

Lowered blood sugar levels have also been linked to insoluble fiber consumption.

While many studies on fiber and diabetes use fiber supplements rather than high-fiber meals, it is still a good idea to increase your fiber intake by eating more fruits and vegetables.

Chapter 3: Shopping List

- Salad greens
- Whole-wheat or legume pasta
- Broccoli
- Whole-grain bread with at least 3 g. of
- Cauliflower
- Squash
- Quinoa
- Green beans
- Wild rice
- Asparagus
- 100% whole-grain or whole-wheat
- Brussel sprouts
- Red, green, orange, or yellow peppers
- Cornmeal
- Onions
- Oatmeal
- Black beans
- Millet
- Lentils
- Amaranth
- White beans
- Barley
- Parmesan, ricotta, or cottage cheese
- Chickpeas
- Kidney beans
- Low-fat or skimmed milk
- Pinto beans
- Plums
- Skinless, boneless chicken breasts
- All berries
- Oranges
- Salmon, sardines, tuna, and other fatty fish
- Peaches
- Tomatoes
- White fish fillets
- Grapefruit
- Skinless turkey breast
- Tofu and tempeh
- Apples
- Tuna
- Pears
- Apricots
- Eggs
- Cherries
- Vinegar
- Olive oil
- Coffee
- Mustard
- Walnuts, almonds, or other raw nuts
- Hot sauces
- Salsa
- Apples
- Tomatoes
- Fresh vegetables
- Corn
- Cucumber
- Fresh basil
- Onion
- Red bell pepper
- Romaine lettuce

Chapter 4: Recipes

BREAKFAST

1. Peanut Butter Toast

Making Duration Period: 5 minutes

Culinary Period: 8 minutes

Number of Portions: 2

Required Material for Recipe:

- 2 pieces of whole wheat toast
- Peanut butter, 2 tablespoons
- 2 bananas, plus cinnamon to taste (about 2 tbsp)

Step By Step Instructions for Recipe:

1. Bananas should be sliced, and the bread should be toasted. Toast some bread with peanut butter, then stack some banana slices on top. Sprinkle some cinnamon on top for flavor.

Nutritional Analysis:

- Quantity of Energy in Calories: 266
- Quantity of fat: 9.3g
- Quantity of carbs: 38.3g
- Quantity of protein: 8.1g
- Quantity of sugar: 7g
- Quantity of sodium: 2mg
- Quantity of GI: 24

2. Crêpe Cakes with Banana

Making Duration Period: 6 minutes

Culinary Period: 18 minutes

Number of Portions: 4

Required Material for Recipe:

- Sprinkle avocado oil for cooking
- Reduced-fat plain cream cheese, about 4 ounces (113 grams)
- Bananas, 2 med.
- 4 big eggs
- Vanilla extract, half a teaspoon
- Salt use only 1/8 teaspoon

Step By Step Instructions for Recipe:

1. Prepare the surface of a big skillet for cooking by heating it for 2–3 minutes over low heat while spraying it with cooking spray. Cream cheese and bananas should be mashed together in a medium basin.
2. Second, pour 2 teaspoons of batter on each cake onto the hot pan and evenly distribute it using the bottom of a big scoop or ladle. Let it cook for 7–9 minutes.
3. Turn the cake over and cook for 1 minute.

Nutritional Analysis:

- Quantity of Energy in Calories: 176
- Quantity of fat: 9.1g
- Quantity of protein: 9.1g
- Quantity of carbs: 15.1g
- Quantity of fiber: 2.1g
- Quantity of sugar: 8.1g
- Quantity of sodium: 214mg

3. Savory Egg Muffins

Making Duration Period: 12 minutes
Culinary Period: 33 minutes
Number of Portions: 6

Required Material for Recipe:

- 1.5 cups of water
- Unsalted Butter, 2 Tablespoons
- Single 6-ounce package of Chicken stuffing mixed with less salt, best for the stovetop
- Bulk Sausage, Pork, 3 oz.

- Spritzing for the stove
- 1.5 oz Shredded Monterey Jack cheese
- One-fourth of a cup of sliced green onions
- 6 beaten eggs
- Half a cup of minced red sweet pepper

Step By Step Instructions for Recipe:

1. Preheat the oven to 400 degrees Fahrenheit.
2. The butter may be melted in anything from 1/2 to 1 cup of water. By putting all the pieces together. Take it off the burner, cover it, and let it sit for five minutes.
3. To fluff the filling, use a pork chop. Ten minutes is all we need.
4. Brown the sausages over medium heat in a small pan while the filling cools. To separate it, just mix.
5. The bottom and edges of 12 greased muffin cups should contain roughly 14 cups of batter.
6. Incorporate 1 egg for every cup of filling. You may top the eggs with cheddar, ham, bell peppers, and green onions if you want.
7. Cook at 400 degrees for 18-20 minutes.
8. Wait five minutes before serving. Use a thin, sharp knife to gently pry apart the glass muffin's edge.
9. Take out the dish and serve.
10. Start serving right away.

Nutritional Analysis:

- Quantity of Energy in Calories: 292
- Quantity of Fat: 16.7 g
- Quantity of Total Carbs: 18 g
- Quantity of Proteins: 14.6 g

- Quantity of Sugar: 3 g
- Quantity of Sodium: 1 mg
- Quantity of GI: 3

4. Pancakes with Blueberry and Peaches

Making Duration Period: 12 minutes
Culinary Period: 16 minutes
Number of Portions: 6
Required Material for Recipe:

- 1 1/2 cups of flour for all purposes
- 2-tablespoons of Splenda
- 2 tablespoons of flaxseed (optional)
- Baking powder, 1 tablespoon
- 1/4 teaspoon table salt
- One and 1/2 cup fat-free buttermilk

- A pinch of grated lemon rind
- 2 eggs
- One cup of blueberries, fresh
- 1 cup of fresh, chopped peaches
- Unsalted Butter, 2 Tablespoons
- half a cup of blueberries, fresh (optional)

Step By Step Instructions for Recipe:

1. Beat the flour, or measure it out with care. With a knife, level.
2. Sift the flour, Splenda and flax seeds, baking powder, and salt into a large basin and mix together with a fork.
3. Buttermilk, lemon zest, and eggs should be mixed together in a small cup using a fork.
4. To barely moisten, combine with the buttermilk mixture and stir. The blueberries and peaches should be folded very thinly.
5. Heat a cast-iron or other nonstick pan over medium heat. Put a third of a cup of flour in the frying pan.
6. Prepare for 2–3 minutes over medium heat, or until the foam thickly covers the surface and the edges become crispy.
7. Slowly turn over the pancake.
8. Prepare for two to three minutes, or until the bottom is golden brown.

Nutritional Analysis:

- Quantity of Energy in Calories: 238
- Quantity of Fat: 2.8 g
- Quantity of Total Carbs: 14 g
- Quantity of Proteins: 8.1 g

- Quantity of Sugar: 3 g
- Quantity of Sodium: 1 mg
- Quantity of GI: 38

5. Potato, Egg, and Sausage Frittata

Making Duration Period: 30 minutes

Culinary Period: 30 minutes

Number of Portions: 4

Required Material for Recipe:

- 2 links of sausage
- a single teaspoon of olive oil
- Four cups of potatoes
- 4 eggs
- 1/4 cup fat-free milk
- 1/4 tsp salt
- Dried Basil Leaves, and oregano 1/8 Teaspoon of each
- 2 cups of tomatoes
- 1/2 cup of a garlic-cheese mixture
- 1 tablespoon of pepper, to taste

Step By Step Instructions for Recipe:

1. Slice each sausage link into eighths. Prepare a 10-inch, oil-coated, nonstick pan for medium heat. Before adding the sausage and potatoes, cook for 6-8 minutes, stirring regularly, or until the root vegetables are golden brown. Blend the egg and milk together in a small bowl using a fork or whisk. The egg mixture should be poured on top of the potato mixture. Cover and simmer over low heat for 5 minutes; after the mixture has begun to harden on the bottom and sides, gently remove cooked portions with a spatula to make room for thin, uncooked bits to flow to the bottom. Don't overcook the eggs; you want them to be slightly thickened but still runny. Salt, basil, oregano, tomatoes, and cheese round out the flavor profile of the eggs. Turn the heat down to low, cover, and let it simmer for 5 minutes, or until the cheese is melted and the center is set. Put in some salt, pepper, and green onion for flavor.

Nutritional Analysis:

- Quantity of Energy in Calories: 500
- Quantity of Fat: 43.5 g
- Quantity of Total Carbs: 56 g
- Quantity of Proteins: 31 g
- Quantity of Sugar: 4 g
- Quantity of Sodium: 4 mg
- Quantity of GI: 36

6. Breakfast Quesadilla

Making Duration Period: 10 minutes

Culinary Period: 2 minutes

Number of Portions: 1

Required Material for Recipe:

- spray for nonstick pans
- Refrigerated Eggs, 1/4 Cup
- One corn tortilla
- Shaved 2 tablespoons of part-skim The term "mozzarella"
- 2 tablespoons black beans
- 2 tablespoons of chopped tomato

Step By Step Instructions for Recipe:

1. Slick frying spray should be used to coat a massive nonstick skillet. Turn the heat on the skillet to medium. Put the egg in the heated pan after seasoning it with the spice blend. The egg will start to set around the edges and on the bottom when it is cooked without stirring over medium heat. Use a paper towel to wipe off the same pan. Coat the pan with nonstick cooking spray. Turn the heat on the skillet to medium. To brown the tortilla and thoroughly cook the contents, fry in a hot skillet for about 2 minutes while rotating once. Extra Pico de Gallo may be added on top.

Nutritional Analysis:

- Quantity of Energy in Calories: 175
- Quantity of Fat: 5.1 g
- Quantity of Total Carbs: 24.2 g
- Net Carbs: 5 g
- Quantity of Proteins: 19.6 g
- Quantity of Sugar: 6 g
- Quantity of Sodium: 5 mg
- Quantity of GI: 56

7. Pear Oatmeal

Making Duration Period: 15 minutes

Culinary Period: 10 minutes

Number of Portions: 1

Required Material for Recipe:

- 1/4 cup of oats, rolled
- 1-1/2 tsp fresh ginger
- 1/4 cup chopped pear
- 1/8 tablespoon cinnamon

Step By Step Instructions for Recipe:

1. Boil the oats as directed on the package. Once the ginger has been added, mix it up well. Top with a pear and serve. Add some cinnamon for flavor.

Nutritional Analysis:

- Quantity of Energy in Calories: 108
- Quantity of Fat: 2 g
- Quantity of Total Carbs: 21 g
- Net Carbs: 0.5 g
- Quantity of Proteins: 3 g
- Quantity of Sugar: 6 g
- Quantity of Sodium: 5 mg
- Quantity of GI: 67

8. Bacon and Tomato Frittata

Making Duration Period: 20 minutes

Culinary Period: 20 minutes

Number of Portions: 4

Required Material for Recipe:

- Eight large eggs
- 1/4 teaspoon of salt-free garlic-and-herb seasoning
- 4 ounces of diced bacon
- two teaspoons of canola oil

- 4 average-sized green onions
- 1/2 cup of chopped celery
- 2 tomatoes
- 1/4 cup cheese
- Sour cream (if you prefer)

Step By Step Instructions for Recipe:

1. In a large bowl, combine the egg product with the garlic and herb spice and whisk to combine. An ovenproof, nonstick skillet of around 10 inches in diameter should be used to heat the oil.
2. After incorporating the onions and celery, reduce the heat to medium and whisk the mixture for 1 minute. We recommend setting the thermostat to a comfortable medium-low. Prepare a baking dish by pouring in the eggs.
3. After 6 to 9 minutes, the uncooked egg mixture will have oozed to the bottom of the pan, at which point you may gently lift the edges of the cooked pieces with a spatula. Turn on the broiler in the oven.
4. You may spice up your frittata with adding bacon, cheese, and tomatoes. Keep the top 4 inches away from the heat and broil for 1-2 minutes, or until the cheese is melted. Before serving, dollop some sour cream on top of each dish.

Nutritional Analysis:

- Quantity of Energy in Calories: 268
- Quantity of Fat: 17.4 g
- Quantity of Total Carbs: 2.8 g
- Quantity of Proteins: 24.3
- Quantity of Sugar: 1.5 g

- Quantity of Sodium: 34 mg
- Quantity of GI: 56

10. Chorizo Mexican Breakfast Pizzas

Making Duration Period: 15 minutes

Culinary Period: 25 minutes

Number of Portions: 4

Required Material for Recipe:

- Chorizo is a sausage, 6 oz.
- 1/4 cup salsa and 2 tortillas
- 1/2 cup chile powder and black beans
- 1/2 a cup of diced tomatoes
- half a cup of corn kernels
- cheese equivalent to a quarter cup
- A tablespoon of chopped cilantro
- Mexican cheese, 2 tsp

Step By Step Instructions for Recipe:

1. Set the temperature to 425 degrees Fahrenheit. Sausage should be cooked for about 5 minutes over medium heat in a pan that's at least 8 inches in diameter until browned. Spread Tortillas out on a single large or two smaller baking sheets. Each one gets 2 tablespoons of salsa. On top, sprinkle the remaining Cheddar cheese, tomatoes, corn, and chorizo. Put it in the oven and let it cook for 8 minutes or until the cheese has melted. Slice into wedges and sprinkle with Mexican cheese and half the cilantro. Prepare and serve immediately.

Nutritional Analysis:

- Quantity of Energy in Calories: 563
- Quantity of Fat: 18 g
- Quantity of Total Carbs: 49 g
- Quantity of Proteins: 56 g
- Quantity of Sodium: 12 mg
- Quantity of GI: 23

11. Breakfast Pizza

Making Duration Period: 10 minutes

Culinary Period: 5 minutes

Number of Portions: 1

Required Material for Recipe:

- spray for nonstick pans
- 4 turkey slices pepperoni
- Green pepper, 2 tablespoons
- 2 tablespoons of mushroom slices
- 2 whites of eggs

- Low-fat milk, 1 tablespoon
- One flat deli roll
- 2 tablesp. pizza sauce
- One slice of low-fat mozzarella
- Tomatoes, sliced (4 pieces)

Step By Step Instructions for Recipe:

1. Put some cooking spray in a small pot and heat it over medium heat. Nearly two minutes are spent cooking pepperoni, mushrooms, and sweet peppers in a pan. The pepperoni mixture should be poured into the saucepan after the egg whites and milk have been mixed together in a small dish. Cook and hold off until the egg white mixture has thickened. Then fold over half of the egg white mixture with a spatula. The egg mixture should be divided in half and spread evenly over the Deli Flat pieces. Put tomato on top if you'd like.

Nutritional Analysis:

- Quantity of Energy in Calories: 218
- Quantity of Fat: 6 g
- Quantity of Total Carbs: 23.2 g
- Net Carbs: 2 g
- Quantity of Proteins: 21 g
- Quantity of Sugar: 6 g
- Quantity of Sodium: 123 mg
- Quantity of GI: 50
- Fibers: 3 g

12. Sweet Potato Frittata

Making Duration Period: 30 minutes

Culinary Period: 30 minutes

Number of Portions: 4

Required Material for Recipe:

- Six big eggs
- Half and Half, one cup
- a pinch of kosher salt
- Pepper, ground, to taste
- Two bowls of sugary spuds
- a tablespoon and a half of olive oil
- Finely cut 2 cups of kale
- 1/2 medium onion + 2 cloves garlic
- 3 ounces of fat-free goat cheese

Step By Step Instructions for Recipe:

1. Your oven has to be preheated to 375 degrees. Whisk together the eggs and the following three ingredients in a large mixing basin. For 8-10 minutes, or until soft and golden, sauté potatoes in 1 tbsp of heated oil in a 10-inch ovenproof nonstick pan. Put away and keep warm. For 3–4 minutes, or until wilted and tender, cook the kale in the remaining 1 tbsp of oil before adding the next two ingredients. Cook the veggies for another three minutes after pouring the egg mixture over them. Goat cheese makes for a great finishing touch on the egg mixture. Ten to fourteen minutes at 350°F should do it.

Nutritional Analysis:

- Quantity of Energy in Calories: 199
- Quantity of Fat: 9 g
- Quantity of Total Carbs: 23.2 g
- Quantity of Sodium: 107 mg
- Quantity of GI: 28
- Quantity of Proteins: 9 g
- Quantity of Sugar: 6 g

13. Apple and Pumpkin Waffles

Making Duration Period: 10 minutes

Culinary Period: 20 minutes

Number of Portions: 6

Required Material for Recipe:

- 2 1/4 cups of all-purpose flour
- 2 tablespoons of granulated sugar
- Baking powder, 1 tablespoon
- 1 teaspoon of cinnamon powder
- Nutmeg, ground, 1 teaspoon
- 4 eggs
- Pure pumpkin purée, 1 1/4 cups
- One apple, prepped by peeling, coring, and coarsely chopping
- 1 tablespoon of coconut oil, melted

Step By Step Instructions for Recipe:

1. The flour, sugar, baking soda, powder, cinnamon, and nutmeg should all be combined in one big basin.
2. Put the eggs and pumpkin in a small dish and mix well.
3. Join the liquids to the dry, and mix until combined.
4. Combine the apple with the batter.
5. Follow the manufacturer's instructions for your waffle maker and cook the waffles until they are done, using melted coconut oil to grease the waffle iron.
6. Start serving right away.

Nutritional Analysis:

- Quantity of Energy in Calories: 232
- Quantity of Fat: 4.1 g
- Quantity of Total Carbs: 40.1 g
- Quantity of Proteins: 10.9 g
- Quantity of Sugar: 5.1 g
- Quantity of Sodium: 120 mg

- Quantity of GI: 32

14. Mushroom Frittata

Making Duration Period: 10 minutes

Culinary Period: 15 minutes

Number of Portions: 4

Required Material for Recipe:

- The equivalent of 8 big eggs
- 1/3 cup fat-free milk
- 1/2 tsp ground mace
- Black pepper and sea salt, 1 tablespoon
- Extra-virgin olive oil, 2 teaspoons

- 4 ounces of dried porcini mushrooms (cremini, oyster, shiitake, portobello, etc.)
- 1/2 cup of chopped red onion
- Garlic, minced, 1 teaspoon
- 1/2 cup of crumbled goat cheese

Step By Step Instructions for Recipe:

1. Get the broiler going.
2. Eggs, milk, and nutmeg go into a medium bowl and get mixed together. Season the egg mixture with a pinch of salt and a few grinds of pepper, then put it aside.
3. Put the oil in an ovenproof skillet and coat the bottom by turning the pan over medium heat.
4. For approximately 7 minutes, or until the onion and garlic are transparent, sauté the mushrooms.
5. After the bottom of the frittata has set, pour in the remaining egg mixture and gently raise the edges of the cooked egg to let the uncooked egg seep beneath.
6. Boil the mixture for about a minute in the skillet, or until the top is firm.
7. After broiling the frittata for 1 minute, sprinkle over the goat cheese and return to the oven.
8. Get it out of the oven! Serve by slicing into four wedges.

Nutritional Analysis:

- Quantity of Energy in Calories: 227
- Quantity of Fat: 15.1 g
- Quantity of Total Carbs: 5.1 g

- Quantity of Proteins: 17.1 g

- Quantity of Sugar: 4.1 g

- Quantity of Sodium: 23 mg
- Quantity of GI: 36

16. Pumpkin Topped Waffles

Making Duration Period: 10 minutes

Culinary Period: 10 minutes

Number of Portions: 1

Required Material for Recipe:

- 1 waffle, 1 tablespoon of pumpkin
- 1/2 ounce of low-fat cream cheese
- Toast 1 teaspoon of walnuts.

Step By Step Instructions for Recipe:

1. Toasting waffles as directed is crucial. Stir the pulp of the pumpkin and cream cheese in a suitable mixing bowl. Chop some walnuts and spread them on the waffle.

Nutritional Analysis:

- Quantity of Energy in Calories: 132
- Quantity of Fat: 7 g
- Quantity of Total Carbs: 15.2 g
- Net Carbs: 5 g
- Quantity of Proteins: 4 g
- Quantity of Sugar: 6 g
- Quantity of Sodium: 23 mg
- Quantity of GI: 19

17. Cinnamon Flaxseed Breakfast Loaf

Making Duration Period: 10 minutes

Culinary Period: 30 minutes

Number of Portions: 6

Required Material for Recipe:

- Golden Flaxseed meal, ground, 1/2 cup
- 1/2 cup almond flour
- cinnamon, ground, 1 tablespoon
- 2 teaspoons of baking soda
- 1/2 teaspoon salt
- Xylitol, 2/3 cup, Eggs, 4,
- 1/2 mug of coconut oil

Step By Step Instructions for Recipe:

1. Add xylitol, cinnamon, cloves, baking powder, salt, and flour to flaxseed meal and mix well. Eggs and cooled coconut oil should be combined separately. Combine the liquid and dry components. Put the batter in an aluminum-lined 6-inch cake pan. Add the steam rack with handles and 1 1/2 cups of water to the inner pot. Place the cake pan on the steam rack and secure the cover. Select "Manual" or "Pressure Cook" and enter a time of 30 minutes. As soon as the float valve lowers, which should not take long, release pressure and remove the lid. When the timer goes off, take the pan out of the Instant Pot® and let the bread cool entirely in there. Slice and serve.

Nutritional Analysis:

- Quantity of Energy in Calories: 334
- Quantity of Fat: 15 g
- Quantity of Total Carbs: 39 g
- Quantity of Proteins: 45 g

- Quantity of Sodium: 130 mg
- Quantity of GI: 8

19. Vegetable Breakfast Bowls

Making Duration Period: 10 minutes

Culinary Period: 16 minutes

Number of Portions: 2

Required Material for Recipe:

- 2 tablespoons avocado oil
- Thinly slice 3 leeks, including both the white and light green parts.
- mushrooms, sliced (8 ounces)
- a pinch of salt and a pinch of pepper
- Two peeled and sliced carrots
- 5 kale leaves, cut Finely minced Half a lemon's juice

Step By Step Instructions for Recipe:

1. Press the Sauté button and add oil to the inner pot. Two minutes later, toss in the mushrooms, leeks, and seasonings. Onions and mushrooms should be cooked in a pan for 10 minutes. Combine the kale, carrots, and lemon juice and mix well. Replace the cover, then choose either the Manual or Pressure setting. Set the timer for 4 minutes and start cooking. As soon as the float valve lowers, which should not take long, release pressure and remove the lid. Serve and enjoy immediately.

Nutritional Analysis:

- Quantity of Energy in Calories: 321
- Quantity of Fat: 7 g
- Quantity of Total Carbs: 22 g
- Quantity of Proteins: 21 g
- Quantity of Sodium: 56 mg
- Quantity of GI: 34

20. Strawberries and Cream Quinoa Porridge

Making Duration Period: 2 minutes

Culinary Period: 1 minute

Number of Portions: 6

Required Material for Recipe:

- 1 1/2 cups quinoa, dry and same cups of water
- Unsweetened, full-fat coconut milk, 13-ounce (1 can)
- Half tsp stevia powder
- Vanilla extract, one teaspoon
- strawberries, sliced (1 cup)
- 1/3 cup shredded coconut, unsweetened

Step By Step Instructions for Recipe:

1. In a fine-mesh strainer, thoroughly wash the quinoa. Add the stevia, vanilla, coconut milk, and water to the quinoa. Maintain a healthy blend. Tighten the cap. Make a Choice: Pressure, or Manual Set a timer for one minute and commence cooking. Rapidly depressurize and open the container's lid. Strawberries add, please. Hold off on serving the quinoa until it has cooled down a little. Sprinkle some coconut on top of each dish.

Nutritional Analysis:

- Quantity of Energy in Calories: 239
- Quantity of Fat: 5 g
- Quantity of Total Carbs: 37 g
- Quantity of Proteins: 24 g
- Quantity of Sodium: 79 mg
- Quantity of GI: 6

21. Stuffed Spinach Chicken

Making Duration Period: 30 minutes

Culinary Period: 20 minutes

Number of Portions: 2

Required Material for Recipe:

- 1 1/2 servings of chopped spinach
- a third of a cup of dried tomatoes cut into julienne
- Grated goat cheese equaling a quarter cup
- 1-tablespoon olive oil
- 1/2 pound of chopped fresh asparagus
- 2 tablespoons of old balsamic vinegar
- Toss in 2 minced cloves of clover
- 1/2 teaspoon pepper 1/4 teaspoon salt
- 6 ounces of boneless, skinless chicken breasts

Step By Step Instructions for Recipe:

1. Prepare an oven temperature of 400 degrees Fahrenheit. Combine spinach, garlic, goat cheese, dried tomatoes, pepper, and salt in a small bowl and mix well. Create a pocket in the center of each chicken breast with a knife. Put in the aforementioned ingredients, then use toothpicks to seal the bag. Put some oil in an ovenproof skillet and heat it over medium. Flip the chicken over while cooking. Bake for approximately 10 minutes at 400 degrees. Toss the chicken with a mixture of asparagus, oil, pepper, and salt. Put in the oven for 10–15 minutes. Put some vinegar on it if you want. Put toothpicks in a wastebasket and serve immediately.

Nutritional Analysis:

- Quantity of Energy in Calories: 347
- Quantity of Fat: 14 g
- Quantity of Total Carbs: 13 g
- Quantity of Proteins: 39 g
- Quantity of Sodium: 76 mg
- Quantity of GI: 16

22. Healthy Chicken Gyros

Making Duration Period: 30 minutes

Culinary Period: 5 minutes

Number of Portions: 6

Required Material for Recipe:

- 1 1/2 pounds of chicken breasts without bones and skin
- Half a cup of lemon pepper brew, without salt
- Three Tablespoons of Mint, Finely Chopped
- Greek yogurt, nonfat (1/2 cup)
- two tablespoons of fresh lemon juice
- Dill weed, 1 teaspoon
- 1 medium cucumber, chopped
- Tomato, medium-sized, chopped: 1
- 1/4 tsp. of chopped onion
- Six pita pockets made from 100% whole wheat pita
- 1/3 cup of grated feta

Step By Step Instructions for Recipe:

1. Put some poultry in a casserole and marinate it in brew and herbs. Chill poultry in the fridge for about 6 hours. Take the poultry out of the concoction and throw it away. Warm up a skillet that won't adhere over moderate heat. Chicken can be cooked for about 4–6 minutes once placed. Make the marinade by whisking together some Greek yogurt, lemon juice, parsley, and garlic powder in a small dish. Put the onion, tomato, and cucumber in a separate dish. Toss some poultry into some pita bread. Cover it with the sauce, vegetables, and Feta. Have fun with the meal!

Nutritional Analysis:

- Quantity of Energy in Calories: 248
- Quantity of Fat: 4 g
- Quantity of Total Carbs: 22 g
- Quantity of Proteins: 30 g
- Quantity of Sodium: 23 mg
- Quantity of GI: 54

23. Root Vegetable Egg Casserole

Making Duration Period: 10 minutes

Culinary Period: 29 minutes

Number of Portions: 4

Required Material for Recipe:

- Vegetable oil, 1 tablespoon
- One small shallot, finely chopped
- Finely sliced radish from 1 small one
- 1 medium-sized turnip, finely chopped after peeling
- Two baby carrots, finely chopped and skinned
- a pinch of kosher salt
- 8 eggs
- One tbsp of Fresh Lemon Juice and the same tbsp Thyme Leaves

Step By Step Instructions for Recipe:

1. Following you've added oil, hit the Sauté option. After a minute, throw in some salt and the chopped onion, radish, potato, and carrots. The vegetables only need to cook for 10 minutes. Make sure you select the Cancel button. In a medium dish, beat together the yolks and the lemon juice. Combine the vegetables and herbs, then stir them in. Fill a 7-cup earthenware container with the coating. The eggs should be poured in. The interior saucepan needs a cup of water and a steam stand. Put together a meal to simmer. Tighten the cap. The Manual or Pressure Cooker duration should be set to 18 minutes. Turn off the stopwatch and wait for the float valve to drop before opening the container. After 5 minutes, cut it into portion sizes and serve.

Nutritional Analysis:

- Quantity of Energy in Calories: 324
- Quantity of Fat: 6 g
- Quantity of Total Carbs: 21 g
- Quantity of Proteins: 12 g
- Quantity of Sodium: 67 mg
- Quantity of GI: 16

24. Pork Chops with Vegetables

Making Duration Period: 9 minutes

Culinary Period: 24 minutes

Number of Portions: 4

Required Material for Recipe:

- 4 pig knuckles
- Specifically: 2 ripe, scarlet peppers
- Topping off 1 big green jalapeno
- Four Mushrooms
- 1 onion
- Four low-fat mozzarella pieces
- The equivalent of 2 tablespoons of salt, or to flavor
- black pepper, to flavor (2 tbsp)
- a tablespoon and a half of olive oil

Step By Step Instructions for Recipe:

1. Salt and pepper the four chops and arrange them on a platter. Place two steaks in the air fryer's cooking tray. Spread out the tomato slices, cheddar cubes, black pepper, onion, and mushroom slices. Include some slick strands. Set the oven fryer to 350 degrees Fahrenheit for 20 minutes. Repeat the steps above with the remaining two pork chops.

Nutritional Analysis:

- Quantity of Energy in Calories: 106
- Quantity of Fat: 3.41 g
- Quantity of Total Carbs: 0 g
- Quantity of Proteins: 20.9 g
- Quantity of Sugar: 6 g
- Quantity of Sodium: 100 mg
- Quantity of GI: 45

25. Spiced Chicken Breast

Making Duration Period: 5 minutes

Culinary Period: 12 minutes

Number of Portions: 1

Required Material for Recipe:

- 0.5 tablespoon of avocado oil
- 1/2 teaspoon of cumin seed
- Smoked paprika, 1/8 teaspoon
- Spicy: 2 tablespoons of chili pepper
- Add 2 tablespoons of salt and freshly ground black pepper to taste.
- 1 (4- oz) poultry breasts without the bones and flesh

Step By Step Instructions for Recipe:

1. The griddle should be heated too about medium. Butter up that barbecue rack!
2. Combine the oil, herbs, salt, and pepper in a small dish. Spread the oil concoction over the chicken breasts.
3. Grill the poultry breasts for four to six minutes per side.
4. To be consumed when hot.

Nutritional Analysis:

- Quantity of Energy in Calories: 144
- Quantity of Fat: 4 g
- Quantity of Total Carbs: 1.1 g
- Quantity of Proteins: 24.4 g
- Quantity of Sugar: 0.1 g
- Quantity of Sodium: 156 mg
- Quantity of GI: 34

26. Taco-Stuffed Bell Peppers

Making Duration Period: 10 minutes

Culinary Period: 15 minutes

Number of Portions: 4

Required Material for Recipe:

- 1 pound of minced meat, 80/20
- 1.25 grams chile pepper
- Cumin, 2 teaspoons
- 1 teaspoon of dried garlic
- 1 teaspoon salt 1/4 teaspoon pepper
- Diced tomatoes, one 10-ounce can, drained
- 4 green jalapenos, middle
- One Cup of Shredded Melted Monterey Jack

Step By Step Instructions for Recipe:

- Brown the minced beef for 7 to 10 minutes in a decent skillet over medium heat. Take the meat out of the pan and pour off the oil. Season the beef with salt, black pepper, cumin, and chile powder before returning the pan to the heat. Chopped tomatoes and rinsed chilies from a can be heated in the frying skillet. Keep cooking for another 3–5 minutes. While the sauce is heating, cut each bell pepper in half lengthwise. The whitish skin and the seeds must go. Sprinkle a quarter cup of cheddar on top of each bell pepper after filling it with the hot concoction. Insert the container containing the filled jalapenos into the air fryer. Time it for about 15 minutes at 350 degrees Fahrenheit. Serve

Nutritional Analysis:

- Quantity of Energy in Calories: 346
- Quantity of Fat: 19 g
- Quantity of Total Carbs: 111 g
- Net Carbs: 1 g
- Quantity of Proteins: 28 g
- Quantity of Sugar: 5 g
- Quantity of Sodium: 129 mg
- Quantity of GI: 26

27. Saucy Beef with Broccoli

Making Duration Period: 10 minutes

Culinary Period: 14 minutes

Number of Portions: 4

Required Material for Recipe:

- a tablespoon and a half of olive oil
- 2 minced garlic cloves
- Thinly cut 1-pound meat sirloin tenderloin
- 1/4 cup low-sodium poultry stock
- Ginger, minced, 2 teaspoons
- 1 Tablespoon of Flax Seed Meal
- 1/2 teaspoon pulverized red pepper flakes 2 tablespoons salt and black pepper to flavor
- 1 medium-sized carrot, finely cut after being skinned
- There should be 2 cups of broccoli stems.
- Thinly cut onion (one)

Step By Step Instructions for Recipe:

1. The garlic should be cooked for about a minute in a decent skillet with 1 tablespoon of oil over medium heat. Add the beef and cook for another four to five minutes, or until caramelized. Using a slanted spatula, move the sirloin to a serving dish. Get rid of any surplus fluids in the pan. In a nice dish, combine the soup with ginger, flax seeds, red pepper flakes, salt, and black pepper. In the same pan, melt the leftover oil over medium heat. The combination of carrots, broccoli, and ginger should be cooked for three to four minutes. Add the beef and onions after 3-4 minutes of tossing. Put the meat combination in a bowl or other suitable container and set it aside to chill. Split the concoction between the four receptacles. Put the sealed packages in the freezer for a day or two. Reheat the meal in the oven right before serving.

Nutritional Analysis:

- Quantity of Energy in Calories: 211
- Quantity of Fat: 15 g
- Quantity of Total Carbs: 7 g
- Net Carbs: 1 g
- Quantity of Proteins: 36 g
- Quantity of Sugar: 2 g
- Quantity of Sodium: 127 mg
- Quantity of GI: 34

28. Thyme Rubbed Tuna

Making Duration Period: 10 minutes

Culinary Period: 8 minutes

Number of Portions: 1

Required Material for Recipe:

- juice of half a lemon
- 1/4 teaspoon olive oil
- 1/2 teaspoon of thyme, 1/2 chopped garlic bulb
- 2 tablespoons of salt, and pepper to flavor
- Tuna fillet, one (6-ounce)

Step By Step Instructions for Recipe:

1. Put the oil, lemon juice, herbs, garlic, salt, and pepper in a Ziploc container. After opening the container, shake it and then add the tuna fillet. Coat with a thorough shaking. Chill in the fridge for almost 30 minutes, stirring periodically. Prepare a medium-high fire on the griddle. The griddle needs to be greased. Remove the tuna from the container and dispose of the marinate. Three to four minutes on each side over high heat will suffice when preparing a tuna fillet. Hold back heat for.

Nutritional Analysis:

- Quantity of Energy in Calories: 215
- Quantity of Fat: 5.1 g
- Quantity of Total Carbs: 1 g
- Quantity of Proteins: 40 g
- Quantity of Sugar: 0.2 g
- Quantity of Sodium: 97 mg
- Quantity of GI: 43

29. Garlic Mixed Shrimp

Making Duration Period: 10 minutes

Culinary Period: 6 minutes

Number of Portions: 1

Required Material for Recipe:

- 1/2 teaspoon olive oil
- 14 pounds of medium-sized shrimp, cleaned and deveined
- 2 tablespoons of salt and freshly ground black pepper, to taste 1 big chopped garlic bulb

Step By Step Instructions for Recipe:

1. Fry the shrimp in 12 tablespoons of the oil in a sauté skillet over medium heat for about 3 minutes per side, turning periodically. Hold back heat for.

Nutritional Analysis:

- Quantity of Energy in Calories: 172
- Quantity of Fat: 8.4 g
- Quantity of Total Carbs: 1 g
- Quantity of Proteins: 24.5 g
- Quantity of Sugar: 0 g
- Quantity of Sodium: 74 mg
- Quantity of GI: 28

30. Glazed Scallops

Making Duration Period: 10 minutes

Culinary Period: 6 minutes

Number of Portions: 1

Required Material for Recipe:

- 14 pound of marine scallops, de-muscled
- Season with salt and pepper, to taste, 2 tablespoons
- 1/2 teaspoon olive oil
- 1 little minced clove of garlic

Step By Step Instructions for Recipe:

1. Sprinkle the scallops with salt and pepper. Twelve tablespoons of the oil should be heated over medium heat in a decent sauté skillet, and the garlic should be cooked for one minute. After adding the scallops to the skillet, cook them for two to three minutes on each side. Hold back heat for.

Nutritional Analysis:

- Quantity of Energy in Calories: 164
- Quantity of Fat: 7.9 g
- Quantity of Total Carbs: 2 g
- Quantity of Proteins: 19.2 g
- Quantity of Sugar: 0 g
- Quantity of Sodium: 58 mg
- Quantity of GI: 37

31. Shrimp Stir Fry

Making Duration Period: 10 minutes

Culinary Period: 10 minutes

Number of Portions: 1

Required Material for Recipe:

- Low-sodium soy sauce, 1 tablespoon
- Balsamic vinegar, 1/4 tablespoons
- 1 teaspoon of erythritol
- 1 quarter teaspoon of arrowroot flour
- 1/8 teaspoon of pulverized red pepper flakes
- 1/2 teaspoon of olive oil
- a quarter of a pound of shrimp that has been skinned and deveined
- a quarter of an onion that has also been julienned and same of shallot that has also been sliced

Step By Step Instructions for Recipe:

1. Soy sauce, vinegar, erythritol, arrowroot flour, ginger, and crushed red pepper flakes should all be mixed together in a nice dish. Set apart. A small high-sided pan is heated to high temperatures and used to stir-fry the bell peppers, onion, and red chile for about one to two minutes. Using the spoon, push the pepper mixture to the outer edge of the wok to make room in the center. Cook the shrimp for about a minute and a half, in a single row in the center of the skillet. After adding the bell pepper mixture, cook the prawns for another two minutes. Add the sauce, and cook for 2–3 minutes while turning occasionally. Remove from fire after adding onion. Hold back heat for then serve.

Nutritional Analysis:

- Quantity of Energy in Calories: 225
- Quantity of Fat: 8.2 g
- Quantity of Total Carbs: 8 g
- Net Carbs: 2 g
- Quantity of Proteins: 27.5 g
- Quantity of Sugar: 2.3 g
- Quantity of Sodium: 90 mg
- Quantity of GI: 52

32. Rice Bowl

Making Duration Period: 30 minutes

Culinary Period: 0 minutes

Number of Portions: 4

Required Material for Recipe:

- One tablespoon of olive oil
- Carrots (two), zucchini (one), and infant portobello mushrooms (half a cup) in medium chunks.
- That's 4 big eggs
- 3 cups of brown rice, once boiled
- The equivalent of one teaspoon of olive oil
- One Cup of Sprouts
- Reduced-sodium soy sauce, 1 tablespoon
- a tablespoon of spicy garlic marinade
- Baby Spinach, 1 Cup
- 1 tablespoon of liquid (water)

Step By Step Instructions for Recipe:

1. Oil should be heated over high heat in a big pan. Vegetables like mushrooms, zucchini, and onions can be added and cooked for about 5 minutes. Cook for some time with bean sprouts, spice garlic, water, soy sauce, and greens. Please put it away. Bring a big pot of water to a boil over high heat. The first step is to boil a raw egg for about 5 minutes after breaking it gently into the water. Scoop the eggs out of the water once they're done cooking. Put some rice in each dish and then cover it with the veggies. Sesame oil should be drizzled on top. Before serving, garnish with a fried egg.

Nutritional Analysis:

- Quantity of Energy in Calories: 305
- Quantity of Fat: 11 g
- Quantity of Total Carbs: 40 g
- Quantity of Sodium: 45 mg
- Quantity of GI: 27
- Quantity of Proteins: 12 g
- Quantity of Sugar: 4 g

33. Nutritious Baked Oysters

Making Duration Period: 10 minutes

Culinary Period: 10 minutes

Number of Portions: 4

Required Material for Recipe:

- Approximately 1.5 tablespoons of olive oil
- Butter, equivalent to one table dollop
- To add taste, use 1 teaspoonful of black pepper.
- Season with a teaspoonful of rock salt.
- A single shallot, thinly cut.
- Dozen Oyster in the shell
- 1/4 teaspoon of ground cardamom from 1 very big orange cardamom
- Panko breadcrumbs, about a quarter cup
- Cut Gala fruit (apple) in half

Step By Step Instructions for Recipe:

- Heat the oil and butter in a pan over medium heat. Sauté the shallots for about 2 minutes after adding them. The diced apple would benefit from a splash of lemon juice. The pan needs an apple and some Panko breadcrumbs. After thoroughly combining, take off the heat. The next step is to mix the pepper and cardamom in a pan. Turn the oven temperature up to 450 degrees Fahrenheit. Spread some rock salt in a shallow roasting dish. Place mussels, cut side down, on a cookie pan over a rock salt. Put in an even amount of the apple puree. Ten minutes in the oven should be sufficient to roast the mussels.

Nutritional Analysis:

- Quantity of Energy in Calories: 150
- Quantity of Fat: 11 g
- Quantity of Total Carbs: 11 g
- Quantity of Proteins: 3 g
- Quantity of Sugar: 8 g
- Quantity of Sodium: 34 mg
- Quantity of GI: 12

34. Parmesan Artichokes

Making Duration Period: 10 minutes

Culinary Period: 10 minutes

Number of Portions: 4

Required Material for Recipe:

- 2 large artichokes
- 2 Tablespoons Coconut Oil
- 2 little eggs
- 1/2 cup grated Parmesan
- 1/4 cups of almond meal
- 1/4 teaspoon crushed red pepper

Step By Step Instructions for Recipe:

- Toss the artichokes in coconut oil before immersing them in the egg. In a dish, combine the ground almonds and Parmesan. Toss in the artichoke hearts, and you're ready to cook. Pepper granules are not required. Prepare oven by preheating to 400 degrees and setting timer for 10 minutes. Fry with two basket tosses. Hold back heat for.

Nutritional Analysis:

- Quantity of Energy in Calories: 187
- Quantity of Fat: 11 g
- Quantity of Total Carbs: 15 g
- Quantity of Proteins: 13 g
- Quantity of Sugar: 7 g
- Quantity of Sodium: 12 mg
- Quantity of GI: 7

35. Lentil Potato Stew

Making Duration Period: 10 minutes
Culinary Period: 30 minutes
Number of Portions: 4
Required Material for Recipe:

- 2 tablespoons avocado oil
- 1/2 cup of chopped onion, 2 cloves of minced garlic, 1 to 1 1/2 tablespoons of salt
- Black pepper, 1 tablespoon
- 1 cup of cooked legumes
- 2 chopped carrots 1 cup of diced potato
- 5 cups veggie stock, 1 celery stem, sliced
- 2 sprigs of oregano, minced 2 sprigs of tarragon, chopped
- 1 light coconut milk (13.5 ounce) can

Step By Step Instructions for Recipe:

1. In a very big broth saucepan, melt the avocado oil over hot to moderate heat. Add the garlic, onion, salt, and pepper (three to five minutes) before the onion is done cooking. Mix in the oregano, tarragon, thyme, and 2 and a half cups of veggie stock with the legumes, carrots, potatoes, celery, and celery leaves. Bring the ingredients to a boil, then reduce the heat to medium and simmer, making careful to turn frequently and add another half cup of veggie stock at a time to maintain a consistent cooking consistency.

2. The potatoes and legumes can be cooked for 20–25 minutes in the liquid provided, or until soft. Turn off the fire and add the coconut milk all at once, whisking constantly. Enjoy 4 servings of broth after pouring.

Nutritional Analysis:

- Quantity of Energy in Calories: 85
- Quantity of Fat: 2 g
- Quantity of Total Carbs: 20 g
- Quantity of Net Carbs: 2 g
- Quantity of Proteins: 3 g
- Quantity of Sugar: 1 g
- Quantity of Fiber: 2 g
- Quantity of Sodium: 45 mg
- Quantity of GI: 18

36. Cider Pork Stew

Making Duration Period: 9 minutes

Culinary Period: 12 hours

Number of Portions: 3

Required Material for Recipe:

- 2 pounds of pork shoulder roast
- 3 potatoes, sliced, medium
- 3 carrots, big
- Slicing 2 medium-sized onions
- Apple, one cup, diced roughly
- 1/2 cup celery (chopped)
- 3 tbsp of a fast-cooking tapioca
- 2 glasses of apple juice
- one teaspoon of salt
- One tsp caraway seeds
- a quarter of a teaspoon of black pepper

Step By Step Instructions for Recipe:

1. Cube the flesh to an inch in size. Combine the tapioca, apple, celery, onion, carrot, potato, and beef in a slow cooker (3.5-5.5 quarts). Mix in apple juice, pepper, caraway seeds, and salt.
2. Ten to twelve hours of slow cooking with the lid on. Use the celery stalks as garnish if you'd like.

Nutritional Analysis:

- Quantity of Energy in Calories: 268
- Quantity of Fat: 10 g
- Quantity of Total Carbs: 26 g
- Quantity of Proteins: 25 g
- Quantity of Sugar: 7 g
- Quantity of Sodium: 34 mg
- Quantity of GI: 35

37. Herbed Chickpea Soup

Making Duration Period: 15 minutes

Culinary Period: 35 minutes

Number of Portions: 2

Required Material for Recipe:

- 1 pound of legumes, boiled
- Vegetables: 1 pound, cut
- Vegetable stock, 1 cup
- Seasoning: 2 tablespoons of a vegetable blend

Step By Step Instructions for Recipe:

1. Put everything you need for the meal into the instant pot and mix well. The broth will take 35 minutes to prepare. Ease the pressure, of course.

Nutritional Analysis:

- Quantity of Energy in Calories: 310
- Quantity of Fat: 5 g
- Quantity of Total Carbs: 20 g
- Quantity of Net Carbs: 2 g
- Quantity of Proteins: 27 g
- Quantity of Sugar: 1 g
- Quantity of Fiber: 2 g
- Quantity of Sodium: 39 mg
- Quantity of GI: 26

38. Fish Fry with Lemon and Parsley

Making Duration Period: 30 minutes

Culinary Period: 20 minutes

Number of Portions: 1

Required Material for Recipe:

- 1 piece of fillet
- 1 tablespoon olive oil and 1 butter
- One Tablespoon of Fresh Lemon Juice
- Miniature sprig of cilantro

Step By Step Instructions for Recipe:

1. Add black pepper and salt to the flesh side of the fish only. Melt the butter and oil together in a pan that won't adhere. Cook for three minutes with the skin side down.
2. Carefully turn and roast for an additional minute or two, based on the width of the piece. (The outer covering may be removed by gentle peeling if desired.) Using a spatula, carefully transfer the plaice to a hot platter, skin side down.
3. Add the lemon juice and cilantro and return the skillet to the stove over medium heat, whisking continuously for a few seconds. Serve the fish with the creamy sauce on the side.

Nutritional Analysis:

- Quantity of Energy in Calories: 207
- Quantity of Fat: 22 g
- Quantity of Total Carbs: 33 g
- Quantity of Proteins: 11 g
- Quantity of Sugar: 2 g
- Quantity of Sodium: 26 mg
- Quantity of GI: 47

39. Tuna with Hoisin Sauce

Making Duration Period: 35 minutes

Culinary Period: 50 minutes

Number of Portions: 1

Required Material for Recipe:

- Tuna fillet weighing 110 grams
- Vegetables for a stir-fry, 300-350 pounds
- 1 tablespoon of coconut oil,
- 2 tablespoons hoisin sauce
- Suggested Use: 1 Tablespoon Crushed Chili

Step By Step Instructions for Recipe:

1. Both pepper and salt should be used to season both surfaces of the tuna. The tuna and veggies should be stir-fried for three to four minutes in a large, oil-filled, Teflon cooking skillet or wok over high heat, or until the tuna is faintly colored.

2. After adding the hoisin sauce, cook for an additional 20-30 seconds before mixing with the salmon and greens. Optional chile peppers can be sprinkled on top before serving.

Nutritional Analysis:

- Quantity of Energy in Calories: 200
- Quantity of Fat: 14 g
- Quantity of Total Carbs: 23 g
- Quantity of Proteins: 9 g
- Quantity of Sugar: 5 g
- Quantity of Sodium: 54 mg
- Quantity of GI: 46

40. Chipotle Chili Pork

Making Duration Period: 4 hours 20 minutes

Culinary Period: 20 minutes

Number of Portions: 4

Required Material for Recipe:

- 4 pork steaks (about 1 inch wide and 5 ounces each)
- Chili sauce, chipotle, 1 tablespoon
- Vim and vigor 1 lime
- 2 tsp of garlic, chopped
- 1 teaspoon of cinnamon powder
- Extra pure olive oil, 1 tablespoon
- 1 tablespoon of salt
- 2 slices of citrus, for decoration

Step By Step Instructions for Recipe:

1. Put everything except the lemon slices into a large dish and mix well. Mix everything together by tossing.
2. Marinate for at least 4 hours in the freezer after placing the plastic-wrapped dish inside.
3. Preheat the oven to 400 degrees Fahrenheit (205 degrees C). Set a tray in a roasting dish.
4. Put the dish in a warm place and wait 15 minutes. After getting rid of the marinate, put the pork on the shelf.
5. In a warm oven, roast for 20 minutes, turning once. Flip the meat over halfway through the grilling time.
6. As soon as possible, bring out the lime slices.

Nutritional Analysis:

- Quantity of Energy in Calories: 204
- Quantity of Fat: 9 g
- Quantity of Total Carbs: 1 g
- Quantity of Proteins: 30 g
- Quantity of Sugar: 1 g
- Quantity of Sodium: 30 mg
- Quantity of GI: 60

Lamb Kofta with Cucumber Salad

Making Duration Period: 10 minutes

Culinary Period: 15 minutes

Number of Portions: 4

Required Material for Recipe:

- 1/2 teaspoon white vinegar
- chili pepper powder, 1 tablespoon
- 1 split teaspoon of marine salt
- Cucumbers (two) and red onion (half) both finely diced

- Lamb meat, 1 pound (454 grams)
- 2 teaspoons of cilantro seed
- 1 teaspoon of cumin seed
- Three chopped garlic cloves
- 1 tablespoon of minced fresh mint

Step By Step Instructions for Recipe:

1. It is recommended that the oven be preheated to 375 degrees Fahrenheit (190 degrees Celsius). If you're using a baking pan with a lip, cover it with parchment paper.
2. A half teaspoon of salt should be added to the dish of vinegar and chli pepper . Cucumbers and onion should be thrown in after they have been added. Set apart.
3. Lamb, coriander, cumin, garlic, mint, and the final 1/2 tsp salt should be mixed together in a big dish. Form the beef into 1-inch patties and place them on the pan.
4. The interior temperature of the lamb should reach 140 degrees Fahrenheit (60 degrees Celsius) after about 15 minutes of roasting.
5. Salad on the side, please.

Nutritional Analysis:

- Quantity of Energy in Calories: 346
- Quantity of Fat: 27 g
- Quantity of Total Carbs: 6 g
- Quantity of Net Carbs: 3 g

- Quantity of Proteins: 20 g
- Quantity of Sugar: 5 g
- Quantity of Sodium: 29 mg
- Quantity of GI: 23

41. Chicken with Balsamic Kale

Making Duration Period: 5 minutes

Culinary Period: 15 minutes

Number of Portions: 4

Required Material for Recipe:

- 4 boneless, skinless chicken breasts (4 ounces / 113 g)
- 1/2 tsp pepper
- coarsely ground black pepper, 1 tablespoon
- Unsalted Butter, 2 Tablespoons
- Extra pure olive oil, 1 tablespoon
- Loosely packed 8 cups of trimmed, coarsely sliced kale (about 2 bunches)
- one-half cup balsamic vinegar
- Toss in 20 sliced cherry tomatoes

Step By Step Instructions for Recipe:

- Sprinkle salt and pepper on both surfaces of the chicken breast. A big saucepan is heated on the stove's middle setting. Oil and butter should be heated. For 8-10 minutes in total cooking time, with the poultry flipped over once. When the poultry is done heating, remove it from the skillet and set it away. Turn the stove to medium heat. Add the peppers to the skillet and simmer for 3 minutes, stirring once a minute. After adding the tomato and vinegar, cook for another three to five minutes. One chicken breast per serving, along with kale, should be divided into four pieces.

Nutritional Analysis:

- Quantity of Energy in Calories: 294
- Quantity of Fat: 11 g
- Quantity of Total Carbs: 17 g
- Quantity of Net Carbs: 12 g
- Quantity of Proteins: 31 g
- Quantity of Sugar: 4 g
- Quantity of Fiber: 3 g
- Quantity of Sodium: 45 mg
- Quantity of GI: 38

42. Baked Asparagus with Bell Peppers

Making Duration Period: 5 minutes

Culinary Period: 15 minutes

Number of Portions: 4

Required Material for Recipe:

- Woody ends removed of 1 pound (454 g) of asparagus sliced into 2-inch pieces.
- 2 peeled and sliced red bell peppers
- 2 tablespoons of Italian sauce; 1 small onion, based

Step By Step Instructions for Recipe:

1. Preheat the oven to 400 degrees Fahrenheit (205 degrees C). A roasting pan lined with parchment paper should then be used.
2. Put the asparagus, peppers, onion, and sauce in a big dish and toss to combine.
3. In a single layer on a cookie pan, broil the vegetables for 15 minutes. Toss the vegetables around with a spoon once during heating.
4. Quickly arrange it on a serving dish and serve.

Nutritional Analysis:

- Quantity of Energy in Calories: 92
- Quantity of Fat: 4.8 g
- Quantity of Total Carbs: 10.7 g
- QuantityNet Carbs: 1 g
- Quantity of Proteins: 2.9 g
- Quantity of Sugar: 5.7 g
- Quantity of Sodium: 56 mg
- Quantity of GI: 33

43. Portobello Mushrooms with Spinach

Making Duration Period: 4 minutes

Culinary Period: 18 minutes

Number of Portions: 4

Required Material for Recipe:

- Eight full-sized Portobello mushrooms
- Three teaspoons of high-quality olive oil, each
- About 4 quarts of raw greens
- 1 medium red bell pepper, chopped; 1/4 cup shredded low-fat feta cheese;

Step By Step Instructions for Recipe:

- Preheat the oven to 450F (235C).
- The chopping surface should be cleared of the mushroom stalks. Take a utensil and scoop out the innards, then throw them away. Spread 2 tablespoons of olive oil over the mushrooms.
- Spread the mushrooms cap-side down on a baking tray. Roast for 20 minutes in an oven that has been warmed to 400 degrees.
- The leftover olive oil should be heated until it shimmers in a skillet over medium heat.
- Add the greens and red bell pepper when the veggies are soft and continue simmering for 8 minutes, turning occasionally. After taking it off the stove, set the skillet inside a dish.
- When the mushrooms are done cooking, remove them from the oven and place them in a plate. Put the vegetables and feta cheese in the mushrooms using a spatula. Reheat the meal just before serving.

Nutritional Analysis:

- Quantity of Energy in Calories: 118
- Quantity of Fat: 6.3 g
- Quantity of Total Carbs: 12.2 g
- Net Carbs: 13.7 g
- Quantity of Proteins: 7.2 g
- Quantity of Sugar: 6.1 g
- Fiber: 4.1 g
- Quantity of Sodium: 89 mg
- Quantity of GI: 42

45. Sautéed Garlicky Cabbage

Making Duration Period: 10 minutes

Culinary Period: 10 minutes

 Number of Portions: 8

Required Material for Recipe:

- 2-tablespoons of high-quality olive oil
- Just one bundle of collard greens, trimmed and sliced thinly
- 1/2 cup of green cabbage, cut thinly with 6 chopped garlic bulbs and 1 tablespoon of low-sodium soy sauce

Step By Step Instructions for Recipe:

- Olive oil should be heated in a large skillet over medium heat. For about 2 minutes, or until they begin to wilt, cook the collard leaves in the oil. Toss the cabbage around. Turn the heat down to medium-low, cover the saucepan, and let the vegetables boil for 5 to 7 minutes, turning periodically. The mixture is then seasoned with garlic and soy sauce and stirred thoroughly. Continue cooking for another 30 seconds, or until a pleasant aroma is produced. Put it on a serving dish after taking it out of the oven.

Nutritional Analysis:

- Quantity of Energy in Calories: 73
- Quantity of Fat: 4.1 g
- Quantity of Total Carbs: 5.9 g
- Net Carbs: 3 g
- Quantity of Proteins: 14.3 g
- Quantity of Sugar: 0 g
- Fiber: 2.9 g
- Quantity of Sodium: 63 mg
- Quantity of GI: 31

46. Spiced Swiss Chard with Cardamom

Making Duration Period: 8 minutes

Culinary Period: 8 minutes

Number of Portions: 4

Required Material for Recipe:

- 2-tablespoons of high-quality olive oil
- Swiss chard, one pound (454 grams), sharp stalks removed, leaves cut
- Chopped kale leaves and gritty stalks from 1 pound (454 grams)
- powdered cardamom, 1/2 tsp
- Freshly strained lemon juice, 1 tablespoon
- Sea salt, 1 tablespoon or to flavor
- black pepper, freshly ground, to taste

Step By Step Instructions for Recipe:

- Olive oil should be heated in a large skillet over medium heat. Swiss chard, kale, cardamom and lemon juice, and salt should all be combined in a pan. For limp leaves, cook for about 10 minutes, turning frequently. After seasoning to suit with salt and pepper, stir well. Greens should be served on a platter while still hot.

Nutritional Analysis:

- Quantity of Energy in Calories: 139
- Quantity of Fat: 6.8 g
- Quantity of Total Carbs: 15.8 g
- Net Carbs: 10.9 g
- Quantity of Proteins: 5.9 g
- Quantity of Sugar: 1 g
- Fiber: 3.9 g
- Quantity of Sodium: 54 mg
- Quantity of GI: 27

47. Flavorful Bok Choy with Almonds

Making Duration Period: 15 minutes

Culinary Period: 7 minutes

Number of Portions: 4

Required Material for Recipe:

- Two Tablespoons of Sesame Oil
- 2 lb. (907 g) bok choy, washed and cut into eighths
- Soy sauce, reduced salt (2 tsp)
- chili pepper powder, 1 tablespoon
- 1/2 cup roasted almond slices

Step By Step Instructions for Recipe:

1. In a deep skillet set over moderate heat, bring the sesame oil to a roaring boil.
2. For about 5 minutes, stirring periodically, sauté the book choy in the hot oil until it is soft but still crunchy. Add the soy sauce and chili pepper after the mixture has been thoroughly combined. When the meal has been sautéed for 2 minutes, move it to a serving platter and top it with chopped almonds.

Nutritional Analysis:

- Quantity of Energy in Calories: 118
- Quantity of Fat: 7.8 g
- Quantity of Total Carbs: 7.9 g
- Net Carbs: 0.8 g
- Quantity of Proteins: 6.2 g
- Quantity of Sugar: 3.0 g
- Fiber: 4.1 g
- Quantity of Sodium: 34 mg
- Quantity of GI: 22

48. Peppery Mushrooms

Making Duration Period: 9 minutes

Culinary Period: 11 minutes

Number of Portions: 4

Required Material for Recipe:

- 1-tablespoon worth of butter
- Extra-virgin olive oil, 2 teaspoons
- 2 kilos of button mushrooms, cut in half
- Garlic, raw, chopped, 2 teaspoons
- 1/4 teaspoon of dried oregano
- 1 tablespoon of sea salt, or to taste
- coarsely ground black pepper, 1 tablespoon

Step By Step Instructions for Recipe:

- In a big pan, melt the olive oil and the butter together over medium heat. Next, put the mushrooms in the skillet and cook them on low heat for about 10 minutes, or until they are tender and slightly browned. Cooking requires frequent stirring. Make sure to give the herbs and garlic a good two minutes in the pan. Put in as much salt and pepper as you like. Inject and savor!

Nutritional Analysis:

- Quantity of Energy in Calories: 97
- Quantity of Fat: 6 g
- Quantity of Total Carbs: 8 g
- Net Carbs: 2 g
- Quantity of Proteins: 7 g
- Quantity of Sugar: 4 g
- Fiber: 2 g

- Quantity of Sodium: 42 mg
- Quantity of GI: 47

49. Carrot Cake Bites

Making Duration Period: 5 minutes

Culinary Period: 15 minutes

Number of Portions: 10

Required Material for Recipe:

- Half tsp cinnamon
- Just one cup dates
- cereals, 1/2 cup
- 2 carrots, big; 1/4 cup chopped nuts
- 1/4 cup of chia seeds
- Turmeric, powdered, 1/4 teaspoons
- Vanilla extract, 1 teaspoon
- 1/2 teaspoon of dried ginger powder
- One quarter tsp salt
- One Tablespoon of Peppercorns

Step By Step Instructions for Recipe:

- Put the dates, grains, nuts, and chia seeds in a food processor and chop them up until everything is evenly distributed. Carrots, turmeric, cardamom, cinnamon, pepper, ginger, and salt should be ground into a puree in a food processor. Form little spheres.

Nutritional Analysis:

- Quantity of Energy in Calories: 48
- Quantity of Fat: 1.7 g
- Quantity of Total Carbs: 8.2 g
- Quantity of Proteins: 0.9 g
- Quantity of Sugar: 6 g
- Quantity of Sodium: 54 mg
- Quantity of GI: 16

50. Plantain Chips

Making Duration Period: 5 minutes

Culinary Period: 15 minutes

Number of Portions: 8

Required Material for Recipe:

- Plantain, verdant, one
- Spray avocado oil (1 tablespoon)
- One-Third of a Teaspoon of Salt

Step By Step Instructions for Recipe:

- To use an air fryer, set the temperature to 375 degrees Fahrenheit. Both edges of the plantain should be trimmed, and the membrane should be sliced along one side. Split the plantain in half lengthwise and peel off the membrane. Make peel segments with a veggie slicer. Spray avocado oil on the air fryer's container. It's important that the plantain pieces in the container don't contact each other. Grease the plantain toast on top. Seven to nine minutes in a hot air fryer is about right. Cook until golden on both sides by flipping the strips over with chopsticks. Immediately sprinkle with salt.

Nutritional Analysis:

- Quantity of Energy in Calories: 109
- Quantity of Fat: 0.3 g
- Quantity of Total Carbs: 28.5 g
- Quantity of Proteins: 1.2 g
- Quantity of Sugar: 3 g
- Quantity of Sodium: 35 mg
- Quantity of GI: 19

51. Garlic Chicken Wings

Making Duration Period: 10 minutes
Culinary Period: 1 hour
Number of Portions: 1
Required Material for Recipe:

- A third of a pound of chicken legs
- A tablespoon and a quarter of pure lemon juice
- 1/4 tsp of each baking powder, ground ginger, raw ginger, minced
- 1/2 tsp chopped garlic,
- Black pepper and salt, to taste, 1 tablespoon

Step By Step Instructions for Recipe:

1. Take off the ends of the wings before you clip them off at the joint. Blend the ginger, garlic, and lemon juice together in a bowl. Toss the chicken wings in the mixture to evenly cover them. Marinate it for at least 15 minutes before serving.

2. Preheat the oven to 250 degrees Fahrenheit. Make sure your oven has a shelf at the bottom. Spray a tray and set it inside a roasting dish.

3. After rinsing the wings in the washbasin, pat them dry with paper napkins.

4. Put the chicken wings in a large zip-top container and add the baking powder, salt, and black pepper. You can cover each well by shaking the container before closing it.

5. Arrange the wings in a single layer on the oven tray. After twenty to thirty minutes, drain the fat from the skillet and continue roasting.

6. When the timer goes off, turn the oven up to 425 degrees Fahrenheit. Bake the wings for 25-30 minutes, or until they reach the desired crispiness and brown color, on a baking tray on the top oven shelf.

7. Start serving right away.

Nutritional Analysis:

- Quantity of Energy in Calories: 292
- Quantity of Fat: 11.3 g
- Quantity of Total Carbs: 1.8 g
- Net Carbs: 1.7 g
- Quantity of Proteins: 43.8 g Quantity of Sugar: 0.1 g
- Fiber: 0.1 g
- Quantity of Sodium: 9 mg
- Quantity of GI: 4

52. Tamari Toasted Almonds

Making Duration Period: 2 minutes
Culinary Period: 8 minutes
Number of Portions: 1

Required Material for Recipe:

- a half cup of uncooked nuts or seeds, such as almonds or sunflowers
- 2 tablespoons of soy sauce (tamari)
- Toasted sesame oil, 1 teaspoon

Step By Step Instructions for Recipe:

1. Almonds should be toasted in a dry pan over medium heat, with frequent turning to prevent browning. After the appropriate amount of time has elapsed for toasting the nuts (7-8 minutes for almonds, or 34 minutes for sunflower seeds), add the tamari and sesame oil and mix to cover the nuts.
2. Turn off the heat, and the tamari combination will dry and adhere to the almonds as they cool.

Nutritional Analysis:

- Quantity of Energy in Calories: 88.7
- Quantity of Fat: 7.5 g
- Quantity of Total Carbs: 3 g
- Quantity of Proteins: 4.5 g
- Quantity of Sugar: 8 g
- Quantity of Sodium: 13 mg
- Quantity of GI: 27

53. Garlic and Cheese Potatoes

Making Duration Period: 7 minutes

Culinary Period: 40 minutes

Number of Portions: 4

Required Material for Recipe:

- Four HALVED Idaho oven potatoes
- 2 cloves of garlic, minced
- salt, to flavor, 1 tablespoon
- 1/2 cup grated cheddar cheese, 1 teaspoon chopped cilantro

Step By Step Instructions for Recipe:

1. Put everything except the cheese in a dish and toss.
2. Spread the potatoes out in a roasting tray and dot with the cheddar. 40 minutes at 390 degrees Fahrenheit.

Nutritional Analysis:

- Quantity of Energy in Calories: 497.5
- Quantity of Fat: 18.7 g
- Quantity of Total Carbs: 66.8 g
- Quantity of Proteins: 16.9 g
- Quantity of Sugar: 3 g
- Quantity of Sodium: 32 mg
- Quantity of GI: 21

54. Cinnamon Spiced Popcorn

Making Duration Period: 10 minutes

Culinary Period: 5 minutes

Number of Portions: 4

Required Material for Recipe:

- 8 tablespoons of microwave popcorn
- a ratio of 1/2 teaspoon sugar to 1 teaspoon cinnamon
- Spray butter taste for cooking

Step By Step Instructions for Recipe:

1. Get a small baking pan ready and preheat the oven to 350 degrees.
2. Prepare the popcorn however you like.
3. In a small dish, combine the sugar and cinnamon, then spread the popcorn out in a baking sheet.
4. Coat the popcorn equally with cooking oil and stir.
5. Add cinnamon and mix once more. To get a slight crunch, cook for 5 minutes; then serve hot.

Nutritional Analysis:

- Quantity of Energy in Calories: 69.5
- Quantity of Fat: 0.7 g
- Quantity of Total Carbs: 14.1 g
- Quantity of Proteins: 2.7 g
- Quantity of Sugar: 1.6 g
- Quantity of Sodium: 43 mg
- Quantity of GI: 21

55. Bacon and Guacamole Fat Bombs

Making Duration Period: 40 minutes

Culinary Period: 15 minutes

Number of Portions: 6

Required Material for Recipe:

- Half an avocado, skinned and cut in half, 1/4 cup butter
- 2 smashed garlic bulbs, 1 minced chile pepper, 2 tablespoons sliced parsley, 1 tablespoon fresh squeezed lime juice
- 1/2 cup of chopped shallot and 4 pieces of bacon
- 1 tablespoon of salt and pepper to flavor

Step By Step Instructions for Recipe:

1. Bake at 375 degrees Fahrenheit, having preheated the oven.
2. Bake the bacon for 15 minutes, in a single layer, on a cookie sheet. Putting aside the oil.
3. Mix the first six items together. Mix in salt and pepper, then taste for seasoning.
4. Mix in the shallot and pork fat. Put in the fridge for about 20 minutes.
5. Make pork crumbs. Form the ingredients into 6 patties.
6. Coat each disk in bacon crumbs.
7. Serve.

Nutritional Analysis:

- Quantity of Energy in Calories: 156
- Quantity of Fat: 15.2 g
- Carb: 1.4 g
- Quantity of Proteins: 3.4 g
- Quantity of Sugar 9 g
- Quantity of Sodium: 23 mg
- Quantity of GI: 43

56. Baked Tortilla Chips

Making Duration Period: 10 minutes

Culinary Period: 15 minutes

Number of Portions: 6

Required Material for Recipe:

- 1 Tablespoon of Oil, Veggie
- Corn tortillas one package
- one teaspoon of salt
- Three Tablespoons of Lime Juice
- Sprinkling of chili pepper
- 1 teaspoon of cumin seed

Step By Step Instructions for Recipe:

1. Your oven has to be preheated to 375 degrees. When all the tortillas have been sliced into eight large sections, arrange them out in a single line on a cookie tray. Mix oil and citrus juice together. Cover all of the tortilla pieces until they are just moist. In a tiny dish, mix the salt, pepper, and cumin. Bake the chips for 7 minutes after covering them in the seasoning concoction. After 8 minutes in the oven, with a halfway rotation of the skillet, the chips should be crunchy but not completely golden. Guacamole and salsa should be served on the side.

Nutritional Analysis:

- Quantity of Energy in Calories: 298
- Quantity of Fat: 4.1 g
- Quantity of Total Carbs: 26 g
- Net Carbs: 20 g
- Quantity of Proteins: 3.3 g
- Quantity of Sugar: 2 g
- Fiber: 4 g
- Quantity of Sodium: 12 mg

- Quantity of GI: 17

57. Popcorns

Making Duration Period: 2 minutes

Culinary Period: 3 minutes

 Number of Portions: 3

Required Material for Recipe:

- Vegetable oil, 1 teaspoon
- 1/2 cup popcorn, unpropped
- 1/2 teaspoon salt

Step By Step Instructions for Recipe:

1. Pop some popcorn and pour some oil over it in a cup. Put the corn in a paper bag and season it with salt. Microwave on high for 2–3 minutes, or until there are 2-second pauses between crackling noises. Remove the sack from the steamer and carefully set it on the serving tray.

Nutritional Analysis:

- Quantity of Energy in Calories: 195
- Quantity of Fat: 3.1 g
- Quantity of Total Carbs: 24.6 g
- Net Carbs: 20 g
- Quantity of Proteins: 4.1 g
- Quantity of Sugar: 0.4 g
- Fiber: 6 g
- Quantity of Sodium: 13 mg
- Quantity of GI: 17

58. Fried Carrot Slices

Making Duration Period: 10 minutes

Culinary Period: 20 minutes

Number of Portions: 1

Required Material for Recipe:

- 3 ounces of carrots, cleaned and sliced crosswise, 1/2 tablespoon of extra-virgin olive oil, and 1/4 teaspoon of arrowroot flour.
- 1/8 teaspoon of dried chilies
- Ground Cinnamon, 1/8 Teaspoon
- Black pepper and salt, to taste, 1 tablespoon

Step By Step Instructions for Recipe:

1. Preheat the oven to 425 degrees Fahrenheit. Line a baking pan with a border with parchment paper before roasting. Put everything in a bowl and stir it up. Bake the carrot spears, turning once, for 20 minutes on a baking pan lined with parchment paper. When you're done, pass the food and enjoy.

Nutritional Analysis:

- Quantity of Energy in Calories: 99
- Quantity of Fat: 7.1 g
- Quantity of Total Carbs: 8 g
- Net Carbs: 5.6 g
- Quantity of Proteins: 0.8 g
- Quantity of Sugar: 4 g
- Fiber: 2.4 g
- Quantity of Sodium: 54 mg
- Quantity of GI: 17

59. Roasted Cinnamon Almonds

Making Duration Period: 5 minutes

Culinary Period: 10 minutes

Number of Portions: 1

Required Material for Recipe:

- Whole Almonds, 2 tablespoons
- cinnamon, ground, 1 tablespoon
- Ground cumin, 1 tablespoon
- 1 tablespoon of cilantro powder
- Black pepper and salt, to taste, 1 tablespoon
- 1/4 teaspoon olive oil

Step By Step Instructions for Recipe:

1. Bake at 350 degrees Fahrenheit; the oven. Combine everything in a large bowl and stir it up. Spread the almond out in a roasting tray lined with parchment paper. Cook at 400 degrees for about 10 minutes, flipping twice. Take them out of the oven and let them cool fully before serving.

Nutritional Analysis:

- Quantity of Energy in Calories: 100
- Quantity of Fat: 8.5 g
- Quantity of Total Carbs: 2.9 g
- Net Carbs: 1.2 g
- Quantity of Proteins: 2.6 g
- Quantity of Sugar: 0.5 g
- Fiber: 1.7 g
- Quantity of Sodium: 19 mg
- Quantity of GI: 13

60. Roasted Peanuts

Making Duration Period: 5 minutes
Culinary Period: 20 minutes
Number of Portions: 1
Required Material for Recipe:

- Raw peanuts, 1 tablespoon salt

Step By Step Instructions for Recipe:

1. Bake at 350 degrees Fahrenheit; the oven. Roast the peanuts for 15 to 20 minutes, spreading them out on a small cookie tray. When the peanuts are done roasting, remove them from the oven and add the salt to a mixing dish. Wait until it's totally cold to serve.

Nutritional Analysis:

- Quantity of Energy in Calories: 155
- Quantity of Fat: 10.5 g
- Quantity of Total Carbs: 4.4 g
- Net Carbs: 2.1 g
- Quantity of Proteins: 0.5 g
- Quantity of Sugar: 1.1 g
- Fiber: 2.3 g
- Quantity of Sodium: 43 mg
- Quantity of GI: 32

61. Cheese Almond Meal Bites

Making Duration Period: 10 minutes
Culinary Period: 2 minutes
Number of Portions: 4

Required Material for Recipe:

- 1/2 cup of shredded Cheddar
- 1 whisked egg ,1/2 teaspoon of salt
- One Cup of Almond Flour
- Coconut oil, 1 teaspoon

Step By Step Instructions for Recipe:

1. Mix the grated cheddar with an egg and some salt and pepper.
2. Using a medium-sized spoon, form the substance into tiny spheres once it has become uniform.
3. Next, roll the spheres in the almond flour to cover them.
4. Coconut oil can be melted in the instant pot by using the sauté setting.
5. The spheres should be cooked for 30 seconds on each side in the instant pot.
6. You should serve the almond flour pieces hot.

Nutritional Analysis:

- Quantity of Energy in Calories: 220
- Quantity of Fat: 18.8 g
- Carb: 5.4 g
- Quantity of Proteins: 9.9 g
- Sugar 6 g
- Quantity of Sodium: 43 mg
- Quantity of GI: 2

62. Salmon and Dill Fat Bombs

Making Duration Period: 35 minutes

Culinary Period: 0 minutes

Number of Portions: 12

Required Material for Recipe:

- 1 pound of cream cheese
- 1/2-pound butter
- 2 ounces (12 box) of cured salmon
- One lemon's worth of liquid
- cilantro, to flavor, 1 tablespoon
- salt, to flavor, 1 tablespoon

Step By Step Instructions for Recipe:

1. Combine all of the explosive components in a blender or food processor.
2. Make bite-sized patties out of the dough and chill them in the fridge for 30 minutes.
3. Eat ice.

Nutritional Analysis:

- Quantity of Energy in Calories: 174
- Quantity of Fat: 13.4 g
- Carb: 0.3 g
- Quantity of Proteins: 3 g
- Quantity of Sugar: 4 g
- Quantity of Sodium: 12 mg
- Quantity of GI: 18

63. Garlicky Kale Chips

Making Duration Period: 5 minutes

Culinary Period: 15 minutes

Number of Portions: 1

Required Material for Recipe:

- 1-fourth of a tablespoon of garlic powder
- Cayenne pepper, 1 tablespoon or to flavor
- 1-tablespoon olive oil
- 1 (8-ounce) bundle Kale, 1/2 tablespoon sea salt, or to taste

Step By Step Instructions for Recipe:

1. Prepare a 355°F oven. Line two oven pans with parchment paper. Add the kale, salt, olive oil, cayenne, and garlic powder to a dish and mix well. Spread the greens out in a single layer on one of the oven pans. Put the pan into the hot oven for 7 minutes. After removing the first baking tray from the oven, transfer the kale to the second sheet and spread it out in a single layer. The spinach layer should be moved around in the oven and baked for another 7 minutes. Appreciate the meal after it's served.

Nutritional Analysis:

- Quantity of Energy in Calories: 116
- Quantity of Fat: 12 g
- Quantity of Total Carbs: 4 g
- Net Carbs: 3 g
- Quantity of Proteins: 12 g
- Quantity of Sugar: 0.5 g
- Fiber: 6 g
- Quantity of Sodium: 34 mg
- Quantity of GI: 56

64. Tomato Mozzarella Skewer

Making Duration Period: 5 minutes

Culinary Period: 5 minutes

Number of Portions: 2

Required Material for Recipe:

- Twelve small tomatoes
- Reduced-fat mozzarella cheese cut into eight 1-inch cubes
- Twelfth basil stems
- Italian Vinaigrette Dressing, Serving Size: 1/4 Cup

Step By Step Instructions for Recipe:

1. Put the tomatoes, cheddar, and bay leaf on separate spears and string them together at random. Caprese spears should be arranged on a big plate and then drizzled with the Italian dressing. Prepare and serve immediately.

Nutritional Analysis:

- Quantity of Energy in Calories: 116
- Quantity of Fat: 12 g
- Quantity of Total Carbs: 4 g
- Net Carbs: 3 g
- Quantity of Proteins: 12 g
- Quantity of Sugar: 0.5 g
- Fiber: 6 g

- Quantity of Sodium: 16 mg
- Quantity of GI: 13

65. Peanut Butter Nuggets

Making Duration Period: 15 minutes

Culinary Period: 60 minutes

Number of Portions: 30

Required Material for Recipe:

- a quarter of a jar of peanut butter
- 1/2 tsp cinnamon powder
- a quarter cup of fat-free milk powder
- One-third cup cereals, One-fourth cup wheat germ
- 1/4 cup coconut, sugar-free
- 1/4 cup apple juice, undiluted

Step By Step Instructions for Recipe:

1. Melt the peanut butter in a skillet and add it to the milk powder and coconut. Whisk together the cereals, apple juice, cinnamon, and wheat germ. Roll the dough into 1-inch patties. The morsels need to be refrigerated and chilled thoroughly before serving.

Nutritional Analysis:

- Quantity of Energy in Calories: 46
- Quantity of Fat: 2.9 g
- Quantity of Total Carbs: 3.8 g

- Quantity of Proteins: 1.9 g
- Quantity of Sugar: 5 g

- Quantity of Sodium: 13 mg
- Quantity of GI: 23

SMOOTHIE

66. Dandelion Avocado Smoothie

Making Duration Period: 15 minutes

Culinary Period: 0 minutes

Number of Portions: 1

Required Material for Recipe:

- Dandelion, 1 cup
- half a cup of coconut water 1 citrus, juiced
- Only one avocado
- Key lime liquid equal to 1

Step By Step Instructions for Recipe:

1. Blend the items in a high-powered mixer until completely homogeneous.

Nutritional Analysis:

- Quantity of Energy in Calories: 160
- Quantity of Fat: 15 g
- Quantity of Total Carbs: 9 g
- Quantity of Proteins: 2 g
- Quantity of Sugar: 5 g
- Quantity of Sodium: 34 mg
- Quantity of GI: 34

67. Amaranth Greens and Avocado Smoothie

Making Duration Period: 15 minutes

Culinary Period: 0 minutes

Number of Portions: 1

Required Material for Recipe:

- One Key Lime, Squeezed
- Apples (two) and avocado (half, pitted)
- Amaranth Greens, 2 Cups
- Just two cups of watercress

Step By Step Instructions for Recipe:

1. Put all of the components, including the skins, in a mixer. Incorporate completely and fully, then blend some more.

Nutritional Analysis:

- Quantity of Energy in Calories: 160
- Quantity of Fat: 15 g
- Quantity of Total Carbs: 9 g

- Quantity of Proteins: 2 g
- Quantity of Sugar: 6 g

- Quantity of Sodium: 45 mg
- Quantity of GI: 47

68. Lettuce, Orange, and Banana Smoothie

Making Duration Period: 15 minutes

Culinary Period: 0 minutes

Number of Portions: 1

Required Material for Recipe:

- 1/2 a head of greens lettuce
- A single big banana
- 1 cup of your favorite berry blend
- 1 citrus, juiced

Step By Step Instructions for Recipe:

1. Start by filling your mixer with citrus juice.
2. Blend the rest of the components in.
3. Enjoy!

Nutritional Analysis:

- Quantity of Energy in Calories: 252.1
- Quantity of Fat: 10 g
- Quantity of Total Carbs: 8 g
- Quantity of Proteins: 4.1 g
- Quantity of Sodium: 56 mg
- Quantity of GI: 60

69. Delicious Elderberry Smoothie

Making Duration Period: 15 minutes

Culinary Period: 0 minutes

Number of Portions: 1

Required Material for Recipe:

- A measure of elderberries, about a cup
- Cucumber, 1 ounce
- Large Apple, One
- one-fourth cup of liquid (water)

Step By Step Instructions for Recipe:

1. Put all the ingredients in a mixer and puree until smooth. Make sure they're perfectly flat by grinding them thoroughly.

Nutritional Analysis:

- Quantity of Energy in Calories: 106
- Quantity of Fat: 25 g
- Quantity of Total Carbs: 26.68 g
- Quantity of Proteins: 9 g
- Quantity of Sugar: 8 g
- Quantity of Sodium: 47 mg
- Quantity of GI: 49

70. Peaches Zucchini Smoothie

Making Duration Period: 15 minutes
Culinary Period: 0 minutes
Number of Portions: 1
Required Material for Recipe:

- 1/2 mug zucchini
- 1/4 cup coconut water,
- Fruit 1/2 cup of each (apricots and peach)

Step By Step Instructions for Recipe:

1. Put all of the ingredients into a mixer and process until completely homogeneous.

Nutritional Analysis:

- Quantity of Energy in Calories: 55
- Quantity of Fat: 0 g
- Quantity of Total Carbs: 14 g
- Quantity of Proteins: 2 g
- Quantity of Sugar: 7 g
- Fiber: 2 g
- Quantity of Sodium: 21 mg
- Quantity of GI: 17

71. Ginger Orange and Strawberry Smoothie

Making Duration Period: 15 minutes
Culinary Period: 0 minutes
Number of Portions: 1
Required Material for Recipe:

- 1 cup of berries
- Juice from one big citrus
- A single big banana
- 1/4 inches of peeled and cut miniature ginger
- Just one cup of water

Step By Step Instructions for Recipe:

1. Orange liquid, please move to the mixer.
2. Mix in the rest of the components until completely uniform.
3. Enjoy!

Nutritional Analysis:

- Quantity of Energy in Calories: 32
- Quantity of Fat: 0.3 g
- Quantity of Total Carbs: 14 g
- Quantity of Proteins: 2 g
- Quantity of Sugar: 8 g
- Fiber: 2 g
- Quantity of Sodium: 10 mg
- Quantity of GI: 15

72. Mango Smoothie

Making Duration Period: 10 minutes

Culinary Period: 0 minutes

Number of Portions: 2

Required Material for Recipe:

- Two Mangoes and 1 banana
- Half tsp vanilla essence
- Almonds, 2 tablespoons and 1 1/2 glasses milk

Step By Step Instructions for Recipe:

- To make a uniform slurry, combine all the components in a food processor. You should be able to achieve a uniform consistency by adding more water if required.

Nutritional Analysis:

- Quantity of Energy in Calories: 205
- Quantity of Fat: 28 g
- Quantity of Total Carbs: 19 g
- Quantity of Proteins: 25 g
- Quantity of Sugar: 7 g
- Quantity of Sodium: 12 mg
- Quantity of GI: 7

73. Strawberry Smoothie

Making Duration Period: 10 minutes

Culinary Period: 0 minutes

Number of Portions: 2

Required Material for Recipe:

- 1 cup of strawberry juice
- Milk, 1 1/2 teaspoons
- Banana, One
- 2.25 tablespoons of nuts

Step By Step Instructions for Recipe:

1. To make a uniform slurry, combine all the components in a food processor. You should be able to achieve a uniform consistency by adding more water if required.

Nutritional Analysis:

- Quantity of Energy in Calories: 267
- Quantity of Fat: 12 g
- Quantity of Total Carbs: 17 g
- Quantity of Proteins: 24 g
- Quantity of Sugar: 4 g
- Quantity of Sodium: 52 mg
- Quantity of GI: 16

74. Mixed Berries Smoothie

Making Duration Period: 10 minutes

Culinary Period: 0 minutes

Number of Portions: 2

Required Material for Recipe:

- 1 cup of strawberry juice
- strawberries, fresh, 1/4 cup
- 1/2 cup cubed ice
- 1/2 a banana
- 1 glass of orange juice

Step By Step Instructions for Recipe:

1. To make a uniform slurry, combine all the components in a food processor. You should be able to achieve a uniform consistency by adding more water if required.

Nutritional Analysis:

- Quantity of Energy in Calories: 177
- Quantity of Fat: 36 g
- Quantity of Total Carbs: 7 g
- Quantity of Proteins: 27 g
- Quantity of Sugar: 3 g
- Quantity of Sodium: 32 mg
- Quantity of GI: 54

75. Apple & Pear Smoothie

Making Duration Period: 10 minutes

Culinary Period: 0 minutes

Number of Portions: 2

Required Material for Recipe:

- Apples, two green
- Two cups of mustard greens, a quarter cup of ice
- 2 peaches; 1/4 teaspoon cinnamon
- Filtered water, 1 1/2 gallons

Step By Step Instructions for Recipe:

1. To make a uniform slurry, combine all the components in a food processor. You should be able to achieve a uniform consistency by adding more water if required.

Nutritional Analysis:

- Quantity of Energy in Calories: 267
- Quantity of Fat: 26 g
- Quantity of Total Carbs: 19 g
- Quantity of Proteins: 25 g
- Quantity of Sugar: 7 g
- Quantity of GI: 76

76. Cantaloupe Smoothie

Making Duration Period: 5 minutes
Culinary Period: 0 minutes
Number of Portions: 2

Required Material for Recipe:

- Cubed melon equals 4 ounces.
- 1/2 liter of beet juice
- 1/2 tsp pepper
- Mixed fruit, cantaloupe spheres, and almonds (1 cup)

Step By Step Instructions for Recipe:

1. Combine the melon, juice, and pepper in a food processor or high-powered mixer. Pulse and combine alternately for 1-2 minutes or until viscous and smooth. Take a moment to mix things up, and then wipe down both surfaces. Alternatively, you can garnish your drink with additional fruit, nuts, herbs, or cherries.

Nutritional Analysis:

- Quantity of Energy in Calories: 135
- Quantity of Fat: 7 g
- Quantity of Total Carbs: 31.2 g
- Quantity of Proteins: 3.4 g
- Quantity of Sugar: 6 g
- Fiber: 3 g
- Quantity of Sodium: 4 mg
- Quantity of GI: 64

77. Pineapple Smoothie

Making Duration Period: 5 minutes

Culinary Period: 0 minutes

Number of Portions: 1

Required Material for Recipe:

- 1 cup of strawberry juice
- Pineapple, diced; almond milk, skim; to serve, refrigerate ingredients.
- Almond butter, 1 tablespoon

Step By Step Instructions for Recipe:

1. Combine all ingredients in a mixer and puree until creamy, adding more almond milk if required. Start serving right away.

Nutritional Analysis:

- Quantity of Energy in Calories: 255
- Quantity of Fat: 11.1 g
- Quantity of Total Carbs: 39.2 g
- Net Carbs: 5 g
- Quantity of Proteins: 5.6 g
- Quantity of Sugar: 6 g
- Fiber: 3 g
- Quantity of Sodium: 30 mg
- Quantity of GI: 43

78. Berry Avocado Smoothie

Making Duration Period: 7 minutes

Culinary Period: 0 minutes

Number of Portions: 2

Required Material for Recipe:

- a single avocado halved
- Strawberry puree, 1 cup
- One-fourth cup of strawberries
- 1/2 mug of fat-free milk
- One-half cup of Greek yogurt

Step By Step Instructions for Recipe:

1. Process the avocado, fruit, and milk in a mixer until smooth.
2. Smooth, silky texture is best when blending fruits.
3. Serve immediately or refrigerate for up to two days.

Nutritional Analysis:

- Quantity of Energy in Calories: 350
- Quantity of Fat: 17 g
- Quantity of Total Carbs: 25 g
- Net Carbs: 15 g
- Quantity of Proteins: 24 g
- Quantity of Sugar: 9 g
- Fiber: 5 g
- Quantity of Sodium: 50 mg
- Quantity of GI: 43

79. Chocolate Avocado Smoothie

Making Duration Period: 5 minutes

Culinary Period: 0 minutes

Number of Portions: 2

Required Material for Recipe:

- Half a mature avocado
- 1/4-liter almond milk
- 3-tablespoons chocolate powder
- Lime juice, 1 teaspoon
- a half a cup of water
- Stevia extract, about 6–7 teaspoons
- 1 tablespoon of salt
- Garnish with 1 tablespoon of fresh mint.

Step By Step Instructions for Recipe:

1. Put everything in a mixer and puree until smooth. Creamy and silky, thanks to a high-speed mix. Sprinkle some fresh mint on top of the drink, and serve.

Nutritional Analysis:

- Quantity of Energy in Calories: 319
- Quantity of Fat: 30 g
- Quantity of Total Carbs: 12 g
- Quantity of Proteins: 2 g
- Quantity of Sugar: 4 g
- Quantity of Sodium: 180 mg
- Quantity of GI: 20

80. Watermelon Smoothie

Making Duration Period: 5 minutes
Culinary Period: 0 minutes
Number of Portions: 4
Required Material for Recipe:

- 5 teaspoons of Stevia extract and 2 cups of sliced watermelon chilling in the fridge
- The Rationale: 1 Lime Juice
- A handful of mint stems
- 1/2 mug of soy milk
- 3 tablespoons of ice

Step By Step Instructions for Recipe:

1. Lime juice, melons, soy milk, Stevia, and mint should all be blended together in a mixer. Use a high-powered blender to make a silky creamy sauce. Put some ice in the mixer, too. Mix the drink with a short pulse and serve right away.

Nutritional Analysis:

- Quantity of Energy in Calories: 33
- Quantity of Fat: 0.5 g
- Quantity of Total Carbs: 6 g
- Quantity of Proteins: 1 g
- Quantity of Sugar: 13 g
- Quantity of Sodium: 13 mg
- Quantity of GI: 42

81. Cinnamon Chia Seed Pudding

Making Duration Period: 5 minutes
Culinary Period: 0 minutes
Number of Portions: 1
Required Material for Recipe:

- To make 3 tablespoons of chia seeds:
- Approximately 1 tsp of maple syrup
- 1/4 teaspoon cinnamon powder
- 3/4 cup plain almond milk
- 1 tablespoon of nuts, sliced

Step By Step Instructions for Recipe:

1. In a tiny glass canister or receptacle, combine almond milk and chia seeds. Shake the container hard after closing it. Give everyone a 5-minute break. Pour some maple syrup and powdered cinnamon into the container. Make sure the seeds don't settle to the bottom of the container by giving it a good jiggle after closing. Marinate for at least four hours in the fridge, preferably overnight. Remove it from the freezer right now. Sprinkle some slivered nuts on top. Enjoy.

Nutritional Analysis:

- Quantity of Energy in Calories: 293
- Quantity of Fat: 17.5 g
- Quantity of Total Carbs: 23 g
- Quantity of Proteins: 12 g
- Quantity of Sugar: 5 g
- Quantity of Sodium: 123 mg

- Quantity of GI: 17

82. Pumpkin Spice Smoothie

Making Duration Period: 5 minutes

Culinary Period: 0 minutes

Number of Portions: 1

Required Material for Recipe:

- Four ice crystals
- 12 cups of toasted almonds
- 1/4 cup honey or sugar
- 1 tablespoon of ground cinnamon
- 1 scoop grams of collagen powder

Step By Step Instructions for Recipe:

1. Put everything into the blender container and whirl it for 20 to 30 seconds. Start serving right now.

Nutritional Analysis:

- Quantity of Energy in Calories: 355
- Quantity of Fat: 26 g
- Quantity of Total Carbs: 8 g
- Quantity of Proteins: 18 g
- Quantity of Sugar: 7 g
- Quantity of Sodium: 235 mg
- Quantity of GI: 24

83. Low-Carb Green Smoothie

Making Duration Period: 5 minutes

Culinary Period: 0 minutes

Number of Portions: 2

Required Material for Recipe:

- Almond butter, 1 tablespoon
- A quarter cup of protein powders and a few teaspoons of Stevia
- 1 cup of pure almond milk
- Vanilla extract, 1 teaspoon
- 1/2 a mango
- Two Cups of Spinach
- Ice crystals, 1 cup

Step By Step Instructions for Recipe:

1. Put everything into the mixer except the ice pieces. Combine and process until uniform. Add ice chunks and blend until completely smooth and buttery.

Nutritional Analysis:

- Quantity of Energy in Calories: 185
- Quantity of Fat: 11 g
- Quantity of Total Carbs: 6 g
- Quantity of Proteins: 16 g
- Quantity of Sugar: 4 g
- Quantity of Sodium: 238 mg
- Quantity of GI: 32

84. Raspberryand Banana Smoothie

Making Duration Period: 5 minutes
Culinary Period: 0 minutes
Number of Portions: 2
Required Material for Recipe:

- Half cup a raspberry
- 1/2 cup organic yogurt
- One large bananas
- Four ice crystals
- 1/2 cup fat-free milk
- 1/2 cup citrus juice, undiluted

Step By Step Instructions for Recipe:

1. All of the components should be cold before use. Washing and peeling fruits is recommended. Blend the fruit, yogurt, milk, and juice together until smooth and velvety using a manual mixer or a smoothie machine. Blend once more after adding the ice chunks. Serve the drink in two cups.

Nutritional Analysis:

- Quantity of Energy in Calories: 114
- Quantity of Fat: 1 g
- Quantity of Total Carbs: 21 g
- Quantity of Proteins: 4 g
- Quantity of Sugar: 7 g
- Quantity of Sodium: 100 mg
- Quantity of GI: 43

85. Kiwi & Cucumber Smoothie

Making Duration Period: 10 minutes

Culinary Period: 0 minutes

Number of Portions: 2

Required Material for Recipe:

- three kiwis
- 2 tablespoons chopped parsley
- Three Drops of Stevia Liquid
- One cucumber
- 1-half teaspoon of ginger
- 2.25 ounces of purified water

Step By Step Instructions for Recipe:

1. To make a uniform slurry, combine all the components in a food processor. You should be able to achieve a uniform consistency by adding more water if required.

Nutritional Analysis:

- Quantity of Energy in Calories: 188
- Quantity of Fat: 14 g
- Quantity of Total Carbs: 13 g
- Quantity of Proteins: 28 g
- Quantity of Sugar: 7 g
- Quantity of Sodium: 23 mg
- Quantity   of   GI: 51

86. Grapes & Kale Smoothie

Making Duration Period: 10 minutes

Culinary Period: 0 minutes

Number of Portions: 2

Required Material for Recipe:

- About 2 tablespoons of greens
- 4 ml of Stevia juice
- Filtered water, 1 1/2 gallons
- 1 cup green grapes, seedless
- 1-tablespoon citrus juice
- ice cubes, 1/4 cup

Step By Step Instructions for Recipe:

1. To make a uniform slurry, combine all the components in a food processor. Add more water until you reach the desired viscosity, which should be a uniform paste.

Nutritional Analysis:

- Quantity of Energy in Calories: 155
- Quantity of Fat: 16 g
- Quantity of Total Carbs: 18 g
- Quantity of Proteins: 34 g
- Quantity of Sugar: 3 g
- Quantity of Sodium: 31 mg
- Quantity of GI: 18

87. Pumpkin Smoothie

Making Duration Period: 10 minutes

Culinary Period: 0 minutes

Number of Portions: 2

Required Material for Recipe:

- Pureed pumpkin, one cup
- Ground flaxseeds, 1 teaspoon
- Almond milk, 1.5 cups
- Banana, One
- Ground cinnamon, 1/4 teaspoons; ice, 1/4 cup

Step By Step Instructions for Recipe:

1. To make a uniform slurry, combine all the components in a food processor. You should be able to achieve a uniform consistency by adding more water if required.

Nutritional Analysis:

- Quantity of Energy in Calories: 207
- Quantity of Fat: 22 g
- Quantity of Total Carbs: 11 g
- Quantity of Proteins: 32 g
- Quantity of Sugar: 9 g
- Quantity of Sodium: 32 mg
- Quantity of GI: 12

DESSERT

88. Flourless Peanut Butter Mug Cake

Making Duration Period: 10 minutes

Culinary Period: 1 minute

Number of Portions: 1

Required Material for Recipe:

- Spreadable peanut butter, 3 tablespoons
- 1 egg, 2 tablespoons of erythritol granules
- Baking Powder, 1/4 Teaspoon
- a pinch of vanilla

Step By Step Instructions for Recipe:

1. Stir the ingredients together firmly with a spatula in a big microwave-safe cup until you have a homogeneous mixture. Put the microwave on high for 1 minute and 30 seconds. Check the cake after 1 minute and modify the heating time according to your microwave's instructions. Wait until the food is heated to serve it.

Nutritional Analysis:

- Quantity of Energy in Calories: 395
- Quantity of Fat: 32.6 g
- Quantity of Total Carbs: 5.1 g
- Quantity of Proteins: 19.4 g
- Quantity of Sugar: 4 g
- Quantity of Sodium: 43 mg
- Quantity of GI: 17

89. Mixed-Berry Cream Tart

Making Duration Period: 20 minutes
Culinary Period: 3 hours 10 minutes
Number of Portions: 8
Required Material for Recipe:

- 2 servings of cherries
- 1/4 cup of cold water
- Strawberries, gelatin, 1 package
- Almond cereal snack packages in sets of three
- 1 cheese-package

- Sugar 1/4 cup, Almond Extract 1/4 teaspoons
- One cup of blueberries, fresh
- 1 cup of whole, ripe strawberries
- 1/4 cup sour cream

Step By Step Instructions for Recipe:

1. In a small dish, use a pastry blender or spatula to mash together 1 cup of the strawberries. Don't eat that additional cup of fruit just yet.

2. Put the water on to boil in a bowl of roughly medium size, and then stir in the gelatin until it has dissolved, about two minutes. Strawberry purée and gelatin go well together. Chill it for 20 minutes in the freezer.

3. While the cereal bars are still in their packaging, crush them with a rolling pin.

4. Create a topping by pressing cereal pieces up the sides of a 9-inch glass pie plate and spreading them out equally across the bottom. The cheese mixture is made by mixing together softened cream cheese, sugar, and almond extract in a small dish. Distribute the crushed oats equally across the dough using a spoonful at a time.

5. Combine the blueberries, raspberries, and strawberry gelatin with the remaining 1 cup of strawberries. Use the cream cheese combination as a garnish and spread it on top. Chill for at least three hours, or until firm. To serve, simply dollop some whipped cream on top.

Nutritional Analysis:

- Quantity of Energy in Calories: 170
- Quantity of Fat: 3 g
- Quantity of Total Carbs: 27 g
- Quantity of Proteins: 8 g

- Quantity of Sugar: 3 g
- Quantity of Sodium: 8 mg
- Quantity of GI: 9

90. Pineapple-Pecan Dessert Squares

Making Duration Period: 22 minutes
Culinary Period: 4 hours 5 minutes
Number of Portions: 18
Required Material for Recipe:

- Water, to Boil, 3/4 Cup
- 1 box of sugar-free lemon jell
- pineapple juice, 1 cup
- one and a half tablespoons of dust
- 1/4 cup coconut 1/2 cup sugar

- 1/2 cup pecans
- butter
- 1 cheese-package
- 1 jar of cream
- 1 pineapple in a can

Step By Step Instructions for Recipe:

1. Boil some water and pour it over the gelatin in a large dish. To ensure that the gelatin is fully incorporated in the pineapple juice, whisk it for about two minutes. Chill the mixture for at least 30 minutes, or until it has the viscosity of syrup.

2. Meanwhile, in a 13x9-inch (3-quart) glass casserole dish, stir together the cracker crumbs, sugar, coconut, pecans, and melted until evenly distributed.

3. To make the garnish, set aside 1/2 cup of the components. Spread the remaining ingredients out evenly across the base of the serving plate.

4. In a separate dish, combine the cream cheese and the remaining cup of sugar and blend with an electric mixer on medium speed until creamy. The cream cheese combination should be folded in until just combined, and the frothy gelatin mixture should be folded in and whipped on high speed until light and airy. Carefully combine the fruit.

5. Empty into a pie dish or other container with a covering and smooth the top. The leftover powder combination, about half a cup, can be used as a garnish. Place in the refrigerator and refrigerate for at least 4 hours. Make six rows and three sections with your meal.

Nutritional Analysis:

- Quantity of Energy in Calories: 120
- Quantity of Fat: 5 g
- Quantity of Total Carbs: 18 g
- Quantity of Proteins: 3 g

- Quantity of Sugar: 6 g
- Quantity of Sodium: 18 mg
- Quantity of GI: 21

91. Cinnamon Bread Pudding

Making Duration Period: 10 minutes

Culinary Period: 45 minutes

Number of Portions: 6

Required Material for Recipe:

- Cubed French or Italian bread that is a day old (4 ounces)
- 2 glasses of nonfat milk

List of pantry staples required:

- 5-tablespoons of Splenda
- One tbsp of cinnamon

- 2 whites of eggs
- 1 egg
- 4 tablespoons of chopped vegan butter

- 1/4 teaspoons pepper and salt
- 1/8 teaspoon of clove powder

Step By Step Instructions for Recipe:

1. Prepare a 350°F oven. In a large pot, bring the milk and vegan butter to a simmer. Turn off the fire after the vegan butter has been completely melted by swirling. Just give it 10 minutes to settle down. Beat the egg whites and yolks separately in a big bowl until foamy. Add in the Splenda, salt, and seasonings. After smoothing out the mixture with a spatula, add the chilled milk and bread. Spread the ingredients out on an oven-safe dish that can contain 1 1/2 cups. Fill the baking skillet with hot water to within an inch of the rack's top. Pudding is done when a utensil placed in the middle comes out clear, usually after 40 to 45 minutes in the oven.

Nutritional Analysis:

- Quantity of Energy in Calories: 362
- Quantity of Fat: 10 g
- Quantity of Total Carbs: 25 g
- Net Carbs: 23 g
- Quantity of Proteins: 14 g

- Quantity of Sugar: 10 g
- Fiber: 2 g
- Quantity of Sodium: 43 mg
- Quantity of GI: 32

92. Chocolate Chip Muffins

Making Duration Period: 10 minutes

Culinary Period: 20 minutes

Number of Portions: 8

Required Material for Recipe:

- 1/4 teaspoon baking powder 1/2 cup coconut flour
- 1/2 tsp salt
- 4 eggs
- a softened 1/3 cup of unsalted butter
- 1/2 cup sugar substitute
- Vanilla essence, 1 tablespoon
- 2 tablespoons coconut cream
- One-third cup of sugar-free chocolate chunks

Step By Step Instructions for Recipe:

1. Prepare a 350F oven.
2. In a dish, combine the coconut flour, baking soda, and salt.
3. Combining the dry components with the wet materials is the next step. Mix the chocolate chunks in gently.
4. Prepare a muffin pan with paper liners and fill them 3/4 full.
5. In the oven for 20 minutes.
6. Serve chilled.

Nutritional Analysis:

- Quantity of Energy in Calories: 168
- Quantity of Fat: 13 g
- Quantity of Total Carbs: 6 g
- Quantity of Proteins: 5 g
- Quantity of Sugar: 5 g
- Quantity of Sodium: 26 mg
- Quantity of GI: 23

93. Peach Custard Tart

Making Duration Period: 5 minutes
Culinary Period: 40 minutes
Number of Portions: 8

Required Material for Recipe:

- Frozen peach chunks, 12 ounces 1 glass of low-fat milk Dissecting 2 Eggs
- 4 teaspoons of vegan butter, sliced and refrigerated

List of pantry staples required:

- 1-cup flour, 3-tablespoon Splenda
- Two or three tablespoons of ice water
- Sugar-free vanilla extract, 1 tablespoon
- 1/8 teaspoon of salt and 1/8 teaspoon of nutmeg,   each

Step By Step Instructions for Recipe:

1. Preheat the oven to 400 degrees Fahrenheit. Flour and 1/4 tbsp salt should be mixed together in a big basin. Use a pastry processor to reduce the plant-based butter to the texture of grainy crumbles. Add cool water, a tablespoon at a time, and combine until the mixture is saturated. Roll out the dough into an 11-inch disk on a lightly floured surface. The removable underside of a 9-inch pie dish should be set on top. Flip the food over and use a utensil to puncture holes in the bottom and corners. Beat one egg white with a spatula in a small dish. To make a flaky top, spread an egg over it. Put the skillet on a cookie tray and bake it for 10 minutes. In a sizable dish, combine the egg whites, Splenda, vanilla, cinnamon, and 1/8 teaspoon of salt. Put the milk in a measuring cup and heat it for a minute in the microwave. Do not bring to a simmer. After the milk has been added, the egg concoction should be covered. Arrange the apricots in the pie shell, and then pour the egg concoction over top. Bake for 25 to 30 minutes, or until the bread is fluffy. Reduce heat until tepid. Cover and refrigerate for at least two hours before serving.

Nutritional Analysis:

- Quantity of Energy in Calories: 180
- Quantity of Fat: 7 g
- Quantity of Total Carbs: 22 g
- Net Carbs: 21 g
- Quantity of Proteins: 5 g
- Quantity of Sugar: 9 g
- Fiber: 1 g
- Quantity of Sodium: 50 mg
- Quantity of GI: 42

94. Raspberry Lemon Cheesecake

Making Duration Period: 5 minutes

Culinary Period: 40 minutes

Number of Portions: 12

Required Material for Recipe:

- 4 ounces of blueberries
- sour cream, nonfat (1 cup)
- 1/4 cup melted fat-free cream cheese
- Egg Replacer, Half a Cup
- two tablespoons of fresh lemon juice
- 2 tablespoons of lemon juice, chopped

List of pantry staples required:

- 1/2 cup plus 3 tablespoons Splenda
- 1/2 cup sugar 1 tablespoon vanilla
- spray for nonstick pans

Step By Step Instructions for Recipe:

1. Prepare a 350F oven. Prepare a square baking sheet, 8 inches in size, with cooking oil. Cream cheese, half a cup of Splenda, and vanilla should be mixed together in a big dish. Combine ingredients by beating at fast speed. After adding the juice and 1 tablespoon of citrus to the cream, beat in the egg substitute. Pour the mixture into the prepared skillet. Wait 40 minutes, or until the dough is solid when touched. When the cake has cooled completely, take it out of the oven. Mix 1 tablespoon of Splenda with the sour cream in a small bowl. Blend ingredients thoroughly by stirring. When the cheesecake has chilled, pour the cream on top. The cake must be refrigerated overnight. Prepare the fruit 30 minutes ahead of time by tossing them with 2 tablespoons of Splenda in a small dish. After the leftover citrus has been incorporated into the fruit concoction, spoon it over the cheesecake. Cut into 12 pieces and serve.

Nutritional Analysis:

- Quantity of Energy in Calories: 114
- Quantity of Fat: 5 g
- Quantity of Total Carbs: 18 g
- Net Carbs: 17 g
- Quantity of Proteins: 3 g

- Quantity of Sugar: 14 g
- Fiber: 1 g
- Quantity of Sodium: 14 mg
- Quantity of GI: 23

95. Raspberry Peach Cobbler

Making Duration Period: 15 minutes
Culinary Period: 40 minutes
Number of Portions: 8
Required Material for Recipe:

- 1 1/4 pounds of peaches, prepped
- Roughly 2.5 pints of perfectly mature blackberries

- One-fourth cup of low-fat buttermilk
- Zest of 1 lemon Two teaspoons of cold plant-based butter, sliced

List of pantry staples required:

- 4 tablespoons + 2 teaspoons Splenda, split 1/2 teaspoon baking powder, and 3/4 cup plus 2 tablespoons flour

- 1/2 teaspoon baking soda
- 0.175 mL sodium
- spray for nonstick pans

-

Step By Step Instructions for Recipe:

1. Raise the temperature of the oven to 425 degrees Fahrenheit. oil a casserole dish that measures 11 by 7 inches with cooking oil.

2. In a large dish, mix together 2 tablespoons of Splenda and 2 tablespoons of flour. Toss the berries and citrus with the flour to cover. Put the fruit in the roasting dish after it has been dusted with flour. After 15 minutes in the oven, you should see the fruit beginning to froth around the sides. The leftover flour, 2 tablespoons of Splenda, salt, baking soda, and baking powder should be combined in a bowl. Mix in vegan butter until the mixture resembles grainy crumbles. The flour combination should be moistened with just enough buttermilk. It's time to remove the fruit from the oven. The buttermilk concoction should be poured over the vegetables as they are cooking. After 18-20 minutes in the oven after the final 2 tsp of Splenda have been added, the top should be lightly toasted. To be consumed when hot

Nutritional Analysis:

- Quantity of Energy in Calories: 130
- Quantity of Fat: 3 g
- Quantity of Total Carbs: 22 g
- Net Carbs: 19 g

- Quantity of Proteins: 2 g
- Quantity of Sugar: 10 g
- Quantity of Sodium: 26 mg
- Quantity of GI: 32

96. Keto Chocolate Bombs

Making Duration Period: 15 minutes

Culinary Period: 0 minutes

Number of Portions: 12

Required Material for Recipe:

- 1/4 cup chocolate powder, unsweetened
- Two Tablespoons of Full-Fat Cream
- Vanilla extract, 1 teaspoon
- Add 2 tablespoons of Stevia
- Peanut butter, 5 tablespoons
- 6-tablespoons of hemp seeds
- 1/2 mug of coconut oil

Step By Step Instructions for Recipe:

1. Combine hemp seeds, cocoa powder, and peanut butter in a big bowl. Blend completely. Combine with the coconut oil to make a thick mixture. Combine the Stevia, vanilla essence, and heavy cream in a large dish. Until a slurry is formed, blend. Roll small disks from the dough. These spheres need to be coated in crushed coconut. Prepare parchment paper on a baking pan. Put them in a roasting dish. Then, chill for about half an hour in the fridge before serving. Ready-to-eat and delicious

Nutritional Analysis:

- Quantity of Energy in Calories: 194
- Quantity of Fat: 16.8 g
- Quantity of Total Carbs: 3.5 g
- Quantity of Proteins: 3.8 g
- Quantity of Sugar: 9 g
- Quantity of Sodium: 23 mg
- Quantity of GI: 56

97. Greek Yogurt Ice Cream

Making Duration Period: 2 hours

Culinary Period: 0 minutes

Number of Portions: 1

Required Material for Recipe:

- 2.25 ounces of fat-free Greek yogurt
- Vanilla extract, 1 teaspoon
- Add 2 tablespoons of Stevia
- Almonds
- Berries
- Vanilla protein powder, .5 ounces
- Unsweetened chocolate powder, 1 teaspoon
- 1/2 cup coconut milk, plain

Step By Step Instructions for Recipe:

1. Smoothie it up by blending some Stevia with some yogurt, protein powder, milk, and chocolate powder. Two hours in the fridge should do the trick. Intermittently stir until the ice cream reaches the desired viscosity. Take it out of the fridge 5 minutes before you plan to serve it.

Nutritional Analysis:

- Quantity of Energy in Calories: 127
- Quantity of Fat: 2.2 g
- Quantity of Total Carbs: 8.1 g
- Quantity of Proteins: 20.1 g
- Quantity of Sugar: 5 g
- Quantity of Sodium: 18 mg
- Quantity of GI: 28

98. Poached Pears

Making Duration Period: 20 minutes

Culinary Period: 1 hour 15 minutes

Number of Portions: 6

Required Material for Recipe:

- Approximately 6 mature pears (about 2 lb.)
- Five glasses of colorless, sugar-free grape juice
- 1/2 a raw lemon juice
- 1/2 of a vanilla bean, cut in half
- Cinnamon stalk, whole, 1"
- 1/2 tsp. dried cranberries

Step By Step Instructions for Recipe:

1. To begin, remove the pears' skins but keep the stalks.
2. In a medium saucepan, combine the liquids, vanilla bean, and cinnamon stick and simmer for a few minutes.
3. Throw in the pears. Pears should be fork-tender after being simmered open for about 30 minutes, during which time they should be turned periodically.
4. Take out the fruit.
5. Strain the reduced liquid after it has simmered for 30–35 minutes.
6. Bring the nectar to room temperature before adding the raisins.
7. Use complex glassware for serving peaches.
8. Spread pears with a layer of raisins and drizzle with honey.

Nutritional Analysis:

- Quantity of Energy in Calories: 79
- Quantity of Fat: 2 g
- Quantity of Total Carbs: 8 g
- Quantity of Proteins: 10 g
- Quantity of Sugar: 2 g
- Quantity of Sodium: 33 mg
- Quantity of GI: 43

99. Delicious Popsicles

Making Duration Period: 5 minutes

Culinary Period: 0 minutes

Number of Portions: 6

Required Material for Recipe:

- 1/4 cup traditional oats
- Juice from one lemon, 4 ounces
- Liquid, 5 droplets Stevia
- 4 ounces of fat-free cottage cheese
- 1 1/2 pounds of fruit

Step By Step Instructions for Recipe:

1. The grains should be ground into a powder in a mixer. Put the Stevia, fruit, cottage cheese, and juice from half a lemon in a dish and stir to combine. Mix it up until it reaches the desired viscosity. Freeze the liquid for about three hours after pouring it into popsicle containers.

Nutritional Analysis:

- Quantity of Energy in Calories: 73
- Quantity of Fat: 0.5 g
- Quantity of Total Carbs: 14.2 g
- Quantity of Proteins: 3.5 g
- Quantity of Sugar: 7 g
- Quantity of Sodium: 23 mg
- Quantity of GI: 47

100. Fruit and Yogurt Parfait

Making Duration Period: 10 minutes

Culinary Period: 0 minutes

Number of Portions: 1

Required Material for Recipe:

- 1/4 cup of blackberries
- 1/4 cup sliced mango
- 1 cup of nonfat Greek yogurt
- One Tablespoon of Flaxseed Meal
- 1/2 cup of low-carb cereal 1/4 cup of chopped strawberries

Step By Step Instructions for Recipe:

1. Half-fill a tiny bowl with yogurt. Arrange the cereal, seeds, and berries in separate layers. Then add another layer of yogurt and another layer of berries and fruits on top of that. Ready-to-eat and delicious

Nutritional Analysis:

- Quantity of Energy in Calories: 388
- Quantity of Fat: 21 g
- Quantity of Total Carbs: 41 g
- Quantity of Proteins: 30 g
- Quantity of Sugar: 7 g
- Quantity of Sodium: 23 mg
- Quantity of GI: 34

101. Banana Cake

Making Duration Period: 10 minutes

Culinary Period: 20 minutes

Number of Portions: 16

Required Material for Recipe:

- 1 1/4 cups chocolate powder and 2 cups flour. unsweetened
- 1/2 teaspoon baking powder
- One big mature banana, pureed, half a cup
- 1/2 a liter of soy milk
- 1/2 cup Splenda Brown Sugar Blend
- 1/4 cup canola oil
- 1 egg
- One Tablespoon of Fresh Lemon Juice
- 1 teaspoon vanilla essence 1/2 cup semisweet dark chocolate chunks

Step By Step Instructions for Recipe:

1. Prepare a 350F oven. Prepare a brownie skillet by lightly spraying it with olive oil cooking spray. In a large dish, whisk together the brown sugar, flour, baking soda, and chocolate. Egg white, soy milk, egg, vanilla, lemon juice, and oil should all be mixed together in a different bowl. In a well-made in the flour, add the dark chocolate chunks and milk. Blend the components together by stirring them together. The mixture should be poured into a greased skillet. After 25 minutes in the oven, check the firmness with your fingers to see if it's done. Serve it on a plate.

Nutritional Analysis:

- Quantity of Energy in Calories: 155
- Quantity of Fat: 4 g
- Quantity of Total Carbs: 27 g
- Quantity of Proteins: 3 g
- Quantity of Sugar: 6 g
- Quantity of Sodium: 18 mg
- Quantity of GI: 67

102. Grapefruit & Lime Yogurt Parfait

Making Duration Period: 10 minutes

Culinary Period: 0 minutes

Number of Portions: 6

Required Material for Recipe:

- Four big scarlet grapefruits
- Four servings of low-fat vanilla yogurt
- 2 teaspoons of shredded lime peel
- The juice of 2 limes, tablespoons
- Three Tablespoons of Honey
- 1 tablespoon of mint leaves, fresh and shredded

Step By Step Instructions for Recipe:

1. Blend the lime juice, lime peel, and yogurt in a big mixing dish. Arrange a quarter of the citrus and a quarter of the yogurt concoction in each parfait bowl. Honey and mint, served with a drizzle.

Nutritional Analysis:

- Quantity of Energy in Calories: 207
- Quantity of Fat: 3 g
- Quantity of Total Carbs: 36 g
- Quantity of Proteins: 10 g
- Quantity of Sugar: 8 g
- Quantity of Sodium: 17 mg
- Quantity of GI: 43

103. Double-Ginger Cookies

Making Duration Period: 45 minutes

Culinary Period: 2 hours

Number of Portions: 5 dozen

Required Material for Recipe:

- 1/4 cup molasses 1/4 cup butter
- 1 egg
- a quarter of a cup of sugar
- 1 and 3/4 ounces of flour
- 1/2 tsp baking powder

- 1/4 teaspoon ginger and cinnamon
- 1/2 tsp pepper
- 1/3 tsp salt
- citrus marmalade, 1/4 cup
- (2 tablespoons) ginger

Step By Step Instructions for Recipe:

1. In a medium dish, whisk or combine together 3/4 cup sugar, butter, egg, and molasses on medium speed. All-purpose flour, baking powder, cinnamon, ginger, cloves, and salt should be combined in a big bowl. Cover and chill for a minimum of 2 hours in the refrigerator.

2. Prepare the oven for baking at 350 degrees Fahrenheit. oil nonstick cooking oil lightly onto baking pans.

3. Take a small, wide dish and load it halfway with sugar. Sugar-coated pastry pieces won't adhere to your hands if you roll them in your palms. Place the spheres in a single layer on a baking tray with about two inches of space between them. Make a dent in the middle of each orb using your finger. Spread the marmalade among the wells to the extent of just under a quarter of a tablespoon.

4. Crystallized ginger makes a lovely finishing touch. Bake at 400 degrees for 8-10 minutes. Transfer to wire cooling racks straight from oven pans. It usually takes me about 30 minutes to cool down completely.

Nutritional Analysis:

- Quantity of Energy in Calories: 87
- Quantity of Fat: 8 g
- Quantity of Total Carbs: 4 g
- Quantity of Proteins: 8 g

- Quantity of Sugar: 9 g
- Quantity of Sodium: 20 mg
- Quantity of GI: 40

104. Sugar-Free White Chocolate

Making Duration Period: 10 minutes

Culinary Period: 5 minutes

Number of Portions: 10

Required Material for Recipe:

- 2. ounces of cocoa powder
- Coconut honey, 2 ounces
- 3 tablespoons of erythritol granules
- The Sweetener Vanilla Stevia, 25 Drops
- 1 tablespoon of salt

Step By Step Instructions for Recipe:

1. In a small pot, melt the cocoa butter in order and coconut honey together over low heat or in the microwave, in 30-second increments. Keep the combination from coming to a simmer. Erythritol, Stevia, and salt should be thoroughly combined. After mixing, transfer to chocolate molds and place in the fridge to set for at least two hours. After use, store it in the refrigerator for up to two weeks in a sealed container.

Nutritional Analysis:

- Quantity of Energy in Calories: 92
- Quantity of Fat: 10 g
- Quantity of Total Carbs: 0.4 g
- Quantity of Proteins: 4.3 g
- Quantity of Sugar: 8 g
- Quantity of Sodium: 31 mg
- Quantity of GI: 5

Chapter 5: 28 Days Meal Plan

DAYS	BREAKFAST	LUNCH/DINNER	DESSERTS/SNACKS
1	Peanut Butter Toast	Cider Pork Stew	Carrot Cake Bites
2	Baked Sweet Potatoes with egg	Beef and Red Bean Chili	Plantain Chips
3	Black Beans and Egg Tacos	Chicken Zucchini Noodle Soup	Almond Chicken Fingers
4	Savory Egg Muffins	Bacon Vegetable Stew	Paprika Buffalo Chicken Wings
5	Pancakes with Blueberry and Peaches	Lentil Potato Stew	Cayenne Broccoli Tots
6	Bulgur Porridge	Parmesan Artichokes	Garlic Chicken Wings
7	Simple Amaranth Porridge	White Zucchini Garlic Rolls	Cheese Spinach Crackers
8	Corn, Egg and Potato Bake	Steamed Mussels	Tamari Toasted Almonds
9	Veggie-Stuffed Omelet	Nutritious Baked Oysters	Garlic and Cheese Potatoes
10	Potato, Egg and Sausage Frittata	Ham with Maple Syrup	Cinnamon Spiced Popcorn

11		Breakfast Quesadilla	Tomatoes and Red Kidney Beans	Bacon and Guacamole Fat Bombs
12		Pear Oatmeal	Pork Fillet	Baked Tortilla Chips
13		Whole-Grain Baby Pancake	Glazed Scallops	Popcorns
14		Bacon and Tomato Frittata	Garlic Mixed Shrimp	Flourless Peanut Butter Mug Cake
15		Chorizo Mexican Breakfast Pizzas	Shrimp Kabobs	Mixed-Berry Cream Tart
16		Breakfast Pizza	Thyme Rubbed Tuna	Pineapple-Pecan Dessert Squares
17		Sweet Potato Frittata	Saucy Beef with Broccoli	Cinnamon Bread Pudding
18		Apple and Pumpkin Waffles	Taco-Stuffed Bell Peppers	Garlic and Cheese Potatoes
19		Buckwheat Crêpes	Spiced Chicken Breast	Almond Chicken Fingers
20		Mushroom Frittata	Turkey Divan Casserole	Pineapple Ice Cream
21		Pumpkin Topped Waffles	Turkey and Quinoa Caprese Casserole	Chocolate Chip Muffins

22	Avocado Toast	Pork Chops with Vegetables	Raspberry Mousse
23	Banana Pancakes	Beef Mushroom Empanadas	Cream Cheese Cookies
24	Cinnamon Flaxseed Breakfast Loaf	Root Vegetable Egg Casserole	Peach Custard Tart
25	Vegetable Breakfast Bowls	Mushroom Tacos	Raspberry Lemon Cheesecake
26	Strawberries and Cream Quinoa Porridge	Healthy Chicken Gyros	Mini Chocolate Cheesecakes
27	Peanut Butter Toast	Stuffed Spinach Chicken	Raspberry Peach Cobbler
28	Baked Sweet Potatoes with egg	Garlic Beef Pasta	Pineapple Ice Cream

Scan the QR code to download 4 printable versions of weekly meal plans.

Conclusion

Thank you for taking the time to read this book. I hope that this book marks the beginning of a journey toward long-term happiness and a vibrant life. Many of the suggestions may be new to you, and we understand that you and those around you may need to make drastic lifestyle changes. It is not always easy to change, but it can be extremely rewarding. It would be a wonderful feeling to see your type 2 diabetes reverse and possibly disappear, especially knowing that you gave your body the nutrients it needed to do its job.

Taking proactive steps to improve your diet and lifestyle may reduce your risk of developing type 2 diabetes significantly. Diabetes can be avoided, but it can also be treated, managed, and even cured. Fortunately, making lifestyle changes may be easier than you think, and a change in the menu does not always imply a life sentence of bland foods that deprive you of all the pleasure you get from your meals and snacks.

It is possible to eat your way to better health and a higher quality of life while having fun along the way. You can take control of your health now and in the future by adhering to a realistic and proven diabetic diet and workout plan that will help your body grow healthier and more resistant to type 2 diabetes.

It is never too late to begin implementing healthy lifestyle changes. The best part about taking control of your daily food and activity levels is that you can not only prevent the onset of type 2 diabetes but also reverse and eliminate current symptoms.

A healthy lifestyle requires eating a well-balanced diet and getting enough exercise on a regular basis. You must learn to balance you're eating and drinking habits with exercise and, if necessary, a diabetes medication.

You'll need to monitor your blood sugar levels on a regular basis. Your doctor will advise you on how frequently you should do it. It's also critical to keep your blood pressure and cholesterol levels within the limits set by your doctor. Make it a habit to schedule your screening exams on a regular basis.

If you are overweight, losing weight, eating fewer calories, and exercising more may help prevent or delay the onset of type 2 diabetes. Treatment for a condition that puts you at risk for type 2 diabetes may help you avoid the disease.

Combining dietary changes with medication prescribed by your doctor is a winning combination. Planning nutritious meals, limiting calories if you're overweight, and staying active are all important aspects of diabetes management. We can live a healthy and long life if we maintain a healthy lifestyle, get regular checkups, and take the proper medications.

With this cookbook, I hope to have given you many ideas for living with your disease more peacefully, and I hope you will want to keep it on hand for each of your recipes.

Best wishes on your journey.

Recipes Index

Printed in Great Britain
by Amazon

22847985R00066